Footnotes
to History

Also by the author:

From the Grass Roots

Footnotes to History

by W. Ernest Thompson

The Naylor Company
Book Publishers of the Southwest
San Antonio, Texas

Library of Congress Cataloging in Publication Data

Thompson, W Ernest. 1878-
   Footnotes to history.

   Includes bibliographical references.
   1. Thompson, W. Ernest, 1878- 2. Texas History. I. Title.
F391.T513   917.64'03'60924   73-19976
ISBN 0-8111-0511-3

This book is dedicated to our many devoted friends
and kindred whose love, loyalty and generosity has
smoothed the pathway for two old people, and
David M. Smith and wife, Charis, who made
publication of the book possible.

Contents

List of Illustrations

Picture section between pages xvi and 1.

Introduction

I have a story to tell because my life has spanned almost a century, embracing two decades of the nineteenth century and seventy-two and a half years of the twentieth century, which has allowed me to witness the living conditions in our part of the country for a longer period than most people.

This story should serve to contribute something of historical interest because it tells of conditions of every day living which are not considered important enough to take place in academic text books, yet should prove of interest to many people who would like to hear about the customs prevailing in those earlier days. I know how it was, because I WAS THERE.

In the first section of *Footnotes to History,* I describe the customs prevailing in most Texas towns, during the last two decades of the nineteenth century, which embraced the years of my childhood, and approaching manhood. Most of which customs were inherited from former dwellers in the states of the Southern Confederacy.

In the second section, I offer a series of short stories and biographies relating to the conditions in the early part of this century which I hope will prove interesting.

Due to the fact that most of the information here presented is based upon recollections of my early life, and the pictures etched upon my brain, a list of authorities is not given in Sections I and II, but when it seems proper to cite authoritative source of material in "After the Sunrise," it is furnished.

The publication of this book was made possible because two very generous and loyal friends, David M. Smith and wife, Charis, believed the story should be told and that it would prove interesting. Generous assistance made it possible and the writing of it was made possible by the help and encouragement of my wife during the sixty-four years of our married life and also to the generous help and loyal encouragement of a host of kindred and friends who have smoothed the paths in the lives of two elderly people in the late afternoon of their lives.

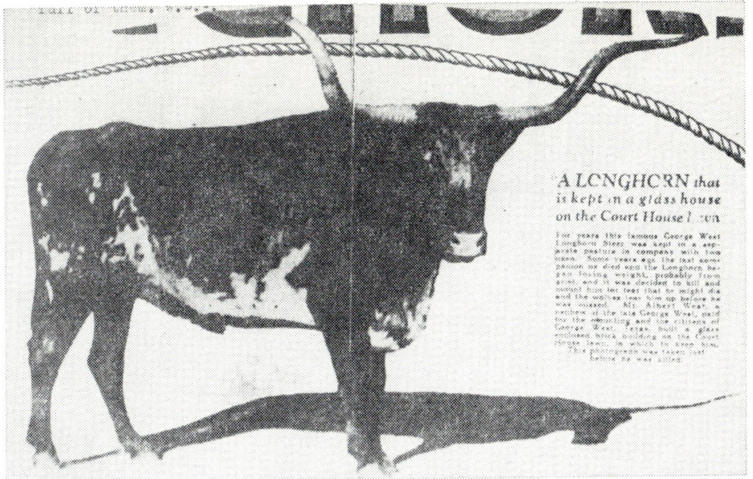

Typical steer that roamed the prairies during the
1880s and 1890s

Type of mule-drawn streetcar used in Dallas
in the 1880s

Pictures taken about 1896, shortly after Dr. Hyer brought the first X-ray machine to the South; lower picture shows Southwestern University faculty from 1895, or before, and later

Southwestern University monthly magazine staff: back row, l to r: B. P. Lane, W. F. Dunkle, J. C. Hardy, W. E. Thompson, J. H. Foster; center row: J. W. Bergin, J. P. Gibbs, J. J. Morgan; front: W. Nelson

M. A. Traylor, fire chief, October 26, 1903   M. A. Traylor, president of the American
to October 23, 1905   Bankers Association

Hill County Grand Jury at turn of the century; standing, l to r: Lon Glan(?), Tom Varnell, Jim Frazier, D. H. Summers, Joe Langford, Bob Poor, Gray Summers; sitting: Mead, Euclid Cox, Tam Brooks, J. R. Thompson, Dee Matthews, Ike Verm(?)

Members of sophomore class at Southwestern University in 1896; only about twenty of these men graduated in 1898 when the author did

IN MY REAR-
VIEW MIRROR

I

In My Rearview Mirror

A Day to Remember

In the early afternoon of April 27, 1972, my wife and I sat in our apartment, while the world was shut out by four walls and a solid roof overhead; the blinds were closed, and a heavy rain was falling outside.

We were fifty miles from the nearest sea water, and yet we saw a man-made miracle happen thousands of miles away, on the face of the broad Pacific.

The heavens opened, and three giant parachutes slowly dropped a great metal car on the waters of that broad ocean. Three whirlybirds hovered over and picked up three bright, fine young men from a rubber boat, near the metal car, and set them down on the deck of the good ship *Ticonderoga*. We watched them as they set foot on the big carrier, after they had spent nearly two weeks encircling the moon or walking on its surface. We heard the ship's chaplain thanking the Almighty God, as he should, for the safe return of these three gallant Americans, whose skill, courage, trained minds and cheerful attitudes had held our attention and our admiration throughout their perilous voyage into outer space. *That was a date we will all remember.*

Other Days to Remember

My wife and I each well remember that evening of October 27, in the year 1908, when we pledged our faith at the altar of the First Methodist Church in Hillsboro, Texas. 22,995 days have passed since that eventful day in our lives, days that bring back other memories of our travels together, as the golden-haired young lady became the beautiful silver-haired companion of riper years. We now live with our todays as well as with our yesterdays.

There are days I do not remember, though I know they happened because my father and the leaf in the Bible told me so. It is said that I arrived at the little town of Fairfield, Freestone County, Texas, on the twenty-fourth day of the third month, in the year 1878, the son of Mrs. Amelia Moreland Thompson and Joseph Rodgers Thompson, and that my wonderful young mother (known only to me later, by her many letters) died in February 1880. And, soon thereafter, I found a home with my mother's widowed sister, Mrs. Rebecca Forrest, and her children, who lived in the valley of the Trinity River, near Midway, in Madison County, Texas, on a farm and ranch.

I know that on a September day, in the year 1880, I was made aware of that place being my home, because my father visited us there then, and, while he and my cousins and I were at the water's edge fishing, my father dived in, swam across the river and back again. You may say, "How can one, at this late date, be sure of the date mentioned?" It is because I clearly remember the incident, and though I believed it was prior to my third birthday, I had no proof of the exact date until I recently found a letter in the mammoth file of letters and news clippings my father and I had saved, in which he had written to some kinspeople that on that date he had visited "Sister Rebecca" and found that Ernest remembered him.

From My Own Cranium

There are records stored away in my noggin showing thousands of pictures of events that have occurred since that day ninety-one and a half years ago. And yet, when the ear specialist had my head X-rayed, the young lady said, "There is nothing in it."

The two and a half years that I still remember as having lived in that home of my beloved Aunt Becky were busy years of a boy who was loved and treated as a baby brother by this queenly lady and her sons.

Between the ages of three and five, I recall having begged cousin Will Forrest to let me ride to the lot on the tall, hard-trotting harness horse, which he had ridden home from town. All went well until the horse headed under a low-hanging tree limb, and I leaned over and fell to the sandy roadside, unhurt, but scared half to death, and crying more from humiliation than pain.

Jousting Cowboys

I enjoyed watching the Madison County cowboys in a tournament as they caught iron rings on their lances, as they charged down the line where the rings were hanging from poles. Each knight, after being properly introduced by the herald, would spear all the rings he could, then salute the queen and king, who sat nearby on a pine platform; then he would dip his lance toward the lady of his choice. The winner's lady became the queen for next year, and he became king.

A Pioneer Preacher

When the family was raking leaves in the front yard and burning them, I was reminded of the fate which would befall bad people in the next world; so I climbed upon a nearby low-lying live oak stump and warned all sinners of the fires of the bad place if they did not mend their evil ways. Yet, I knew no bad people, as the people I knew were of the stuff by which angels were later made. I must have remembered some of the fire and brimstone preached at the Midway Church.

A Skunk Who Came to Dinner

I remember being asked at the dinner table (at noon, of course) to go to the smokehouse and get some salt. As I reached down into the barrel, my hand touched something soft and fluffy, and peeping over, I saw it was a polecat, and so reported.

This resulted in a family council at the smokehouse. When the barrel was turned over, a large, mixed breed dog drew away when the furry animal came out of the barrel, but the little rat terrier dashed in, grabbed the varmint by the neck and soon shook it to death. We had lost our appetite by then.

Leaving the Nest

At the age of five years, Aunt Becky and two of her young sons and I rode in a covered wagon from home to visit Aunt Lora and Uncle Jim Caldwell, who lived on a sheep ranch between Marlin and Waco, where we saw a saddle horse tied to a hitching post at the front gate get stung to death by a swarm of bees. Its owner, then visiting the home, was so badly stung that nursing was needed for quite a spell. And the legend is that a romance then ended.

Transplanted in a New Home

Then came my father to take me to our new home in Hillsboro. I remember a night under a mosquito bar in the Waco Hotel, and a trip the next day, in a mixed passenger and freight train, over the newly laid rails of the M.K.&T. Railroad to Hillsboro, thirty miles north.

From that day in 1883 to one April day in 1923, when my wife and I moved to San Antonio, I called Hillsboro my home, though many of those years were spent elsewhere, either in college or on a West Texas farm and ranch or in San Antonio, for a short spell.

Other Yesterdays

Having described the beginning of that bridge to yesterday, and the yesterday in 1972, when the Apollo Sixteen and its crew completed their moon mission, I may now hop, skip and jump through many of the 33,397 days that I remember, since that September day in 1880.

As the World Turns

In a long life, an old one is astonished at the changing patterns of life and its customs, and even the face of "The Good Earth" is changed so that one who has spent half a century driving over all his state's 254 counties would have difficulty finding his way home now over the scarred landscape after the engineers have cut down the hills, lifted the valley floors, wiped out landmarks, replaced the winding, scenic drives with broad freeways which lead to destruction, and built elevated worms which "puzzle the will." This leads one to wonder at what God had wrought and now what man has done to the face of this beautiful planet.

In the 1880s

The Texas I knew then was a giant cattle range, with farms here and there near little towns, clinging to the newly laid rails to avoid sticking in the mud or the deep sand. In the springtime the timbered hills of East Texas and the prairies of central and western Texas were ablaze with flowers gendered by the varied soils and seasons. There were bluebonnets, Indian paintbrush, wine-cups, dogwood blooms, and magnolias to sweet-scented huisache, and all along the scattered herds of longhorns grazed. The dust was settling on the Chisholm and other northbound cattle trails as the railroads nosed their way across the wide spaces, and furnished cattle cars for the drovers to fill.

My Best Remembered Incidents

Thanksgiving, Christmas, Fourth of July, our birthdays,

and June Teenth, the day that school was out, and circus day were the special days, of course.

The fire fighters had to pull the fire trucks, or an engine if there was one, by hand, before horses were used. If a residence caught fire, the hook-and-ladder truck was pulled up to the house where a human chain was formed, using the rubber buckets, suspended from the sides of the truck, to carry water from the shallow, dug wells to the burning structure. If the fire was on courthouse square, water was pumped by the fire engine from one or both of two deep underground, brick cisterns on each side of the courthouse. When my father's hardware store caught fire, in later years, we had to hurry to get the black powder and dynamite out of the store in a hurry. Peter Mittenthal kept beer on hand in his adjoining grocery store, and opened the keg for the hardworking firemen.

On Friday afternoons, books were closed and it was a period of change and entertainment, such as having story-telling, or declamations, or a spelling contest, each *scholar* seeking to reach the first in the line.

Curfew Must Always Ring at Night and in the Morning

In the mid-1880s, one of our public schoolteachers, named Jim Clark, came from Tennessee with most of his staff with him: a Mr. Horton, who, in afteryears, became governor of Tennessee, and two young ladies.

He introduced bell ringing, in order to regulate the study habits of the students. The big bell clanged at 9:00 P.M. each five nights a week of school, and at 5:00 A.M. This plan was not universally popular with either parents or children, but no strong protest was made.

At the end of his term of service of a year or two, he induced many families to let him take a son or a daughter, or both, back to Winchester, Tennessee, where he and his brother conducted the "Winchester Normal." I happened to be one of them; my parents thought the change of climate might be helpful, in the fine mountain air. Several of us stayed at one boardinghouse, operated by a motherly lady, Mrs. Fuller, who presented me, a twelve-year-old boy, with a silver drinking cup when we were leaving for home.

Pollution Endured

We had a good taste of pollution when we took a train ride on the crude passenger cars. There were open platforms between each car, so that when the conductor, porter, brakeman or butcher boy opened the door, the smoke and cinders filled the car, and in the summertime the windows had to be opened for ventilation. A red-bellied stove in the end of the car did its best to keep some of the passengers warm during the winter months. Then, too, every store, home, church, schoolhouse, and gin kept the home fires burning, as the "chimblies" poured out the smoke from the wood fires.

Merchandising

Some of the clerks came to the stores by not later than six-thirty or seven. Each swept out his store, then dragged some of the stock out to the sidewalk, such as fresh fruit and "Western butter" by the grocers. Hardware men exhibited such items as stoves, lard cans, or specialty articles, so as to attract the attention of the passerby. Barbed wire was in strong demand then, so my father had it stacked in the warehouse as high as a man could reach, all being one-hundred-pound spools. On one occasion a seedy, listless-looking man came into the store and asked, "What's your 'bob' wire worth?" He was told the price was five cents a pound. Then he said, "Smith-Tomlinson has a better price." As the custom in our area then was to bargain, if need be, he was told that if a big enough order was wanted, the price might be shaved a little and was asked about how many spools he would want. "A carload" was the answer, and he was asked his name. Then he said that it was Ferguson, who lived in the Brandon community, and was known as perhaps the richest man in the county, so the pencil pusher really got busy and closed the deal.

Church Time

We three well-scrubbed boys, wearing blacked shoes and Sunday clothes, walked single file toward the First Methodist Church to get to Sunday school by 9:30 A.M., as the warning bells rang from churches all over town. After the superintendent had called the house to order, the secretary would be called on to read the minutes of the last meeting, which was almost a copy of each of several during the year, each group was allowed to seek his class, all being in the main auditorium, and each occupying a separate niche.

After Sunday school we waited outside for a few minutes for the rest of the family to drive up in the surrey; then the family entered the center aisle together.

It was the custom for older people and families to sit in the center aisle, the single men, and often young married men, to sit in the right tier, and the single ladies, and some young married ones, to use the aisle on the left as one entered.

A few members of the Board of Stewards acted as collectors, using velvet bags attached to the end of a stick. My father and Sheriff John Cox usually served in this capacity, they being leaders in the building and operating the church business matters. The preachers were fundamentalists, then. Their mission was to serve the needs of the members of the flock, save souls of men. The Baptists had very fixed ideas regarding immersion, and followed all tenets of their creed. If you got out of line, you might be thrown to lions. One prominent lawyer was charged with drunkenness and, he said, thrown out of the church. What made him mad was "that old drunkard, Dave D., prosecuted me." He and the lawyer prosecutor were also old Confeds and fellow lawyers. The defendant averred that "if he had been charged with fornication he would have pleaded guilty."

TWILIGHT OF A CENTURY

II

Twilight of a Century

Night and Day, Day and Night

Our day began when we heard the meat boy call out
"MEAT BOY," as he galloped by and put the steak, wrap-
ped in heavy brown paper, on the gate post. We knew he
was coming when Gyp began his barking.

Then, if our cow was dry, the milkman would stop and
draw from one of the big cans in front of him the required
amount of sweet milk, buttermilk or cream. He had a specially built hack, with a big can for sweet milk and one for
buttermilk, and a small can in between for cream. The
money would be put in the tin pail we put on the gate
post the night before.

As we got up we could tell whether or not the neighbors
were astir by watching for the smoke from the chimneys,
and hearing the coffee mill grinding and the calf bawling
for his breakfast.

Until some of the boys got bigger, Pa usually started the
fire in the fireplace in the bedroom, and if Suzie was work-

ing for us, she would come early enough to start the fire in the kitchen cookstove. Then, with a fire in the dining room, we were open for business, and we were all busy. At least the two older boys were, and I followed in a few years to take over where they left off.

There was wood to saw or cut, stock to feed, hogs to slop, and boys to dress for school, before we all sat down together for breakfast. Pa left for the store fairly early, though not as early as the clerks did, as they were to start the fires at the store, sweep out, and put samples of merchandise out on the sidewalk, such as the new "Quick Meal Gasoline Stove," or anything that would indicate that this was a hardware store.

We scampered off to school as soon as we could so as to play awhile before classes began.

In the summertime there was plenty to do, too. As soon as the wild mustang grapes were ripe, the women would take us to the Frazier's grove and have us climb up and gather grapes for the jelly to fill the mason jars, and whenever the dewberry season opened, we would go get our baskets full and take on a mass of chiggers.

When the peaches were ready for preserving, there was plenty to do, for Pa had a wonderful selection of peaches of every breed; perhaps we might buy some also. Pa furnished us with every modern gadget known to man to aid in the housework; one of these was the peach peeler that made the job fun for a small boy. At the end of a metal arm was a thin disc of steel, about the size of a thumbnail, which travelled over the surface of the peach, cutting the thinnest peel possible in uniform width and thickness, as I turned the handle of a wheel. There was a coil spring on the arm that held the disc, which caused the proper pressure to be applied. Soon crocks and jars were full of peaches and pears preserved, and peelings were used to make peach jelly. Some of the peaches were dried by being put on top of the house to sun, laid out on shingles.

We had the best water system in town. Due to the fact that most of the wells in town were shallow, the water was not only hard, but not very pure, as the horse and cow lots were near; so Pa had a brick underground cistern into which nothing but pure clean water flowed. He would usually fill it in the wintertime, letting the first hard showers wash off the roof of the house, and then as the water flowed from the gutters, it passed through a tin sifter, and from that to a specially prepared box about three feet deep, filled with gravel, sand and charcoal, and on top of the box was spread a sheet of gauzelike cloth, for further screening.

To keep the water from becoming stagnant, a bucket pump brought the water up on an endless chain, and poured it into a big iron kitchen sink, and from that back into the cistern, unless a bucket was used to catch it. Later, he built an overhead galvanized tank for rainwater to wash with it. But it was hot and not palatable like the cool cistern water.

About suppertime we had to hitch up the buggy horse to the surrey so that the family might take a drive in the cool of the evening. Keep in mind that evening was that period of time between dinnertime (at noon) and suppertime. After supper was "night." There were three meals every day, breakfast, dinner and supper. After I was grown and some of my girl friends came back from Chicago, we had to explain to each other when we had a date the meaning of "after dinner," "in the evening," and similar expressions.

Between Suppertime and Dawn, in the Old Hometown

After supper we would probably go for a drive in the surrey with its grey fringed top, behind old Jim, our first big buggy horse, and later, behind old Roan. My heart suffered much pain when old Roan was sold years later, even though I was a pretty big boy then.

On returning from the drive, we would sit on the front gallery, and watch the firefly spectacle, and have Pa tell about his early experiences in East Texas, after he came to the state in 1865. He had some close calls with rough men in those days, but though he was only five feet seven inches tall, and weighed about 140 pounds, he could hold his own, as he had cool courage and stood his ground.

When we had company, I really enjoyed these sessions, as I would usually sit on the edge of the gallery to be close to the speaker, and listen until I got sleepy, then might stretch out and take a nap. I really enjoyed hearing some ex-Confederate soldier talk. My father was too young to get in the army when he lived in Alabama, as he was only twelve years old when the war started. He was left an orphan during that time.

When bedtime came, everybody got under the mosquito bars and slept, as the houses were not screened.

There was little to disturb our sleep except cats' courtship or fights, and the fire alarm. That is when business picked up. Nothing was so exciting as the dang-a-lang of the fire bell in the dead of night, which called for hasty dressing and a rush to the fire. The equipment was pulled by men instead of horses for a long time. If the fire was in one of the stores, water would be drawn from one of the two big underground cisterns on the square, one on the east side and one on the west side. If a home burned, the well in the yard furnished the water, while all the furniture was piled on the street.

The hook-and-ladder truck carried a string of rubber buckets along the underside of the truck, which made it possible for a human chain to form a bucket brigade, passing these buckets on from hand to hand. Later, a fire engine was used, and still later, horses were used to pull the equipment.

Another night sound that might awaken us was hearing some scavenger men cleaning out the "Backhouse," which was done about once a month. Though the garbage man still has an unsavory job, it is not as bad as these men had.

In the autumn, the sound of cotton wagons clucking their way to gin or back was an encouraging sound, as all business depended upon the cotton yield and the price of the staple. And so life went until the meat boy yelled and the rooster crowed at dawn.

Medicine Chest

Every well-ordered home had a drug department available for most any ordinary ills, such as colds, chapped hands, cuts and bruises of bare feet, biliousness, catarrh, colic, earache, and malaria.

Castor oil led the list, as a thorough cleansing of the system often seemed necessary, and to tell the truth, when I was middle-aged, I found that a generous dose of that stuff was followed by the clearing of a bad case of sore throat or tonsilitis. Castor oil also was needed to grease the buggy axles.

Turpentine was always available when one cut his bare foot on a glass bottle, or stuck a nail in it. Then, Pa would put sugar and turpentine on the cut and wrap a white rag around it, and the wounded boy would continue to play, but walked on his heels for a day or two.

Quinine was used to relieve colds, and perhaps fever, though I am not sure just what else, except malaria.

Mutton suet rubbed on sore places or chapped hands did the trick. Mentholatum now takes its place.

Paregoric was needed for the children with colic or for folks with loose bowels.

Laudanum and sweet oil were useful in case of an earache, or "rising" in the ear.

Wizard Oil was recommended for many skin ailments, and after I rubbed it on my hands the warts soon disappeared.

Sasafras tea was needed in the spring to thin the blood and get the system ready for the warm weather to come.

Calomel was often prescribed by the doctor for moving the liver. Here, too, I found it beneficial when Dr. Bui prescribed a double-barrel dose of it for my neuralgia, later called sinus, which had pained me for a week and the darn stuff cleared up next day. Now, what have you got to say?

Castoria for the babies came into its own when it came on the market.

Doubtless there were other regular items which I have

failed to remember, but most households could get by until the doctor came with the above on hand.

My Hometown

The location and description of Hill County has heretofore been given. Now, I'll record my recollections of the town of Hillsboro as it appeared during the decade between 1880 and 1890. My memory and knowledge goes back only to 1883, however. The population was about two thousand.

Hillsboro was on a black part of the prairie, level except at its boundaries near the creek, where it sloped enough for drainage. Hackberry Creek ran along its northern border, and turned left at the western side where it formed a general border on the west.

Like "All Gaul," the town was divided into three parts. Most of the better homes, and there were no fine ones, were along Elm and Franklin streets, running eastward from the Courthouse Square. Here were the homes of most of the merchants, lawyers, doctors and preachers.

South of this area lay "freetown," as the darkies called it, though some of the white boys called it either Freetown or "Nigger Town." This was an area of rather shabby shacks where all the Negroes lived except those few who lived in servants' houses on the premises of their employers.

Across the railroad tracks were the cotton gins, and later, the oil mill, compress, and cotton factory. The residents were mostly of the laboring class, and that area was known to all of us boys as "Arkansas." Now and then, when the family demanded a change, or the economic status improved, there would be a move over on our side of the tracks. Up and down Waco Street, which ran north and south and formed the eastern side of the Courthouse Square, were some substantial homes too.

The business section started just east of the railroad station and the M.K.&T depot, and ran east a short distance to the Courthouse Square. The most active business was on the south side of Elm from the depot to and along Elm (the south side of the square) and along Waco Street's east line facing the east side of the courthouse. There were a few places of business a block or so extending beyond the square.

The courthouse during the 1880s was a two-story red brick building, topped by a cupola, and above that a staff with a big, red brass ball on it. Hitching racks surrounded the building. The county jail was on the northwest corner of the square. The sheriff made his home in the two-story brick jail. This building was at the same location that a hotel later appeared, then known as the Wear Hotel. Later, the name was changed to Newman. I do not know what the name is now.

Near the square on Franklin Street was the log calaboose, where the village drunks were left to sleep it off. On one occasion, a drunk set fire to his blanket, and had to do some tall yelling to get relief.

Our Home, Yard and Garden
The House:

Our house was a little above the average on the street, being built along the customary lines of that day. It had only two bedrooms when built, but in the course of time, four other rooms were added. Two of these were bedrooms, extending to the west, and a servant's room and an adjoining storage room, or smokehouse, on the north of the back gallery, making the gallery into an enclosed runway. A hall extended through the house, with bedrooms on the east side of it, and parlor, dining room and kitchen on the west of it.

While we were quite small, a trundle bed served me, and I believe the older boys slept in a bed in the dining room, for sometimes a bed would be in that room, especially if company came. Later, Pa built a lean-to, a small bedroom for us three boys. And, at a still later date, it was converted into a bathroom when two more bedrooms were added.

The parlor was a sacred place, to be carefully protected from the natural vandalism of boys running through it.

19

It was usually kept closed except when in use. The first grate installed in the fireplace was in the parlor, which gave it a more attractive appearance than an old-fashioned fireplace. But, either grate or fireplace burnt your shins while your back froze.

In the center of the room was the marble-top table, on which rested the big family Bible, the photograph album, and a stereopticon outfit, with accompanying slides. Of course, there was the upright piano, and the handsome hanging lamp over the marble-top table. A big shade supported long crystals that tinkled when a person walked rapidly across the room. The lamp was on a chain so that it could be lowered for filling and wick trimming. It had a big round wick.

Our houses did not have double floors, but plain pine flooring; so a house got mighty cold when a norther blew under the house, requiring us to put hay under the carpets. The house had a fairly steep roof which gave it a longer life than some these days. Carpenters were very thorough in their work then. Green outside shutters provided privacy and some degree of warmth in winter.

Yard and Garden:

The lot was one hundred feet wide, which was customary, and all yards were enclosed with fences. Our front fence was of white palings, and on the west side of the yard and on the north side was a solid board white-washed fence of upright one-by-twelve planks, six feet high, giving privacy to our backyard and garden. The horse and cow lots were on the northeast corner of the lot, and the buggy shed on the alley running along the east line of the place. The privy, or backhouse, was in the northwest corner. Pa built a plank sidewalk to it, and a latticework supported a grape arbor protecting it. He always had a good garden, with rows of blackberries along the fence. In the front yard a heavy turf of Bermuda grass kept us out of the mud. The front yard was bordered by symmetrical umbrella china trees, which were later replaced by transplanted hackberrys that in a few years made the street one of the best shaded ones anywhere. Pa's selection of peaches, pears and plums was unexcelled. There were trees in the front yard, and some in the backyard. Corded firewood lay along the back fence, with a kindling pile of white pine pieces of varying lengths.

Streets, Roads and Sidewalks

We talk about transportation problems today, but conditions were really rugged in our day. As Hillsboro was in the middle of the black waxy belt, heavy winter rains almost stopped traffic, for the streets and roads would get so boggy that at times I have seen four horses drawing the front wheels of a farmer's wagon, when he came to town to get a sack of flour. In fact, as late as 1906, when my patrician mother-in-law moved to Hillsboro, she felt so sorry for the horses drawing the cab that she wanted to get out and walk for the mud was so deep. It was not only deep, but it was truly waxy. As a very little boy, I wanted to be rich enough to pave the streets with rock. My recollection is that a few blocks in Dallas were then so paved, though most of the small amount of paving even in that city of twenty thousand was of bois d'arc blocks.

Where sidewalks existed, they were either plank or gravel. Some places had no walks, or the gravel had been buried in the mud, requiring us to hold to the fence and step from one high point to another. A few years changed much of the above described trouble.

In the summer we suffered less from the mud, as the roads would dry out faster than in the winter, but they would often become so rutted that they almost became one-way streets or roads. When quite dry, they would at times become hard and glazed, making for fast travel. Later on, with much use, the streets would get inches deep in fine, limestone dust that made housekeeping a headache.

The Courthouse Square was improved some after 1890, when the new courthouse was built, and the brickbats from the old red courthouse were spread over the streets, and later gravel piled on that. But it all would, in the course of time, get lost in the black mud. But these repeated coats of brickbats and gravel furnished such a good foundation for a later built pavement that it has given longer wear than any other pavement in Texas, despite the local traffic, and the streams of traffic that merged the Dallas-to-Waco with the Fort Worth-to-Waco routes.

The dependable route of transportation was by rail, and every year during the last two decades of the nineteenth century saw more and more extension of railroad mileage, as immigration was constant. Every road had its immigration agent as well as its agricultural agent. Our outlet, up until the Dallas branch of the M.K.&T. was built, depended upon the main line that ran south from Forth Worth, through Hillsboro to Waco. To go to Dallas, one had to go to Fort Worth and catch the Texas and Pacific line to Dallas. In later years, the Cotton Belt Tap was built from Corsicana, and the Trinity and Brazos Valley from Cleburne, through Hillsboro, to Mexia, and south. Still later, the most convenient of all was the Interurban from Dallas to Waco. When I say dependable, I do not mean that they ran on schedule, but they could go in any weather.

Spring Cleaning — Also, Fall Cleaning

What a headache springtime brought. The carpets had to be taken up and hung on the fence or the clothesline, and beaten, and beaten, and swept before being put away for the summer. To do this meant getting down on the floor and pulling up thousands of tacks; then when the carpets were removed, the dirty hay or straw underneath had to be either burned or put in the cow shed or the horse stall for bedding. It was too dusty to feed the animals.

Then fresh new prairie hay was laid evenly on the floor after the floor had been scrubbed and mopped with lye soap and water. After the hay was carefully spread, the cool matting would be laid, and a thousand tacks around all the edges held it in place. Next fall, the same thing had to be done in reverse. Another big spring cleaning job

was to air the mattresses, and paint the joints and edges of
the bedstead to get rid of the bedbugs.

Household Equipment (Supplement)

Foot scraper — In this black waxy town, every house must
have a foot scraper on each end of one of the doorsteps, to
scrape the mud off one's feet or shoes or overshoes.

Fly brush — Another active implement was the fly brush.
Sometimes it would be a brush off the peach tree, but the
long peacock-feather brush was usually used, especially
when company came. This meant that someone at the table
had to spend much of the time fanning the flies away, and
that often fell to the lot of my stepmother, who combined
that duty with seeing that the guests were properly
served.

Hat rack — The item now lacking in so many modern homes
was a fixture in our home — the hat rack, or hall tree. This
was in the wide hall that separated the parlor, dining room
and kitchen from the bedrooms. Some of the hooks were
metal or, sometimes, buffalo horns, flanking a mirror perhaps, and underneath this was a sort of cabinet with a
hinged top for overshoes. On the side of the hat rack was
the umbrella stand, an upright cylinder for holding parasols
and umbrellas, which were in much use. My father needed
it in rainy weather, and, because his fair skin would sunburn
easily, he used it in hot weather.

Milk-cooling system — My father, who never overlooked
any apparatus to make housekeeping less burdensome, had
two parallel troughs made that he would fill with water,
and between them, and below, was a twelve-inch plank on
which would rest milk cans in cloth sacks. The sacks had
long lips that lapped over into the trough on each side and
kept the bags wet, so that the wind blowing over them kept
the milk cool. This outfit was on the back porch, near the

open hallway door, so that the south breeze coming through the hall would reach it. Every home also had an icebox and a kitchen safe. Instead of roasting green coffee in a biscuit pan, he had an iron sphere with a handle that was over one eye of the cookstove, and we could whirl it easier than the old way. We had the first gasoline cookstove, the first fuelless cooker, and other household inventions.

When Shadows Fall

When death invaded the home, the shadows were really dark, but the helpful, sympathetic neighbors helped to relieve the distress as much as possible. The ladies would take over much of the housework in the home so bereaved. The undertaker, who was a furniture dealer, would prepare the body and leave it at the home. At night, the neighbors would gather and sit for awhile, then one or two couples usually would "sit up" with the corpse until about 1:00 A.M., when two to four other persons would relieve them and sit until daylight. Then, some neighbor woman would come in and cook breakfast for the family. One custom was to put a silver coin over each eye of the corpse.

The services were held at the church, and often a long burial service with, sometimes, a sermon. The hearse was drawn by two to four jet black horses with stiff upright black plumes on their bridles. The pallbearers would walk in front of the hearse, two abreast, to the graveside, and after the service they would aid others in filling the grave The church bell would keep up a continuous tolling while the procession was on the way to the cemetery.

The men of the bereaved family would wear black arm bands for some time after the death. I think about a month, but do not remember how long a period custom expected it to be done. The widow would wear black clothes and a black hat with mourning veil for quite a long period.

The problem of the widow's survival, in the days when men carried little life insurance, was often solved by the lady taking in boarders, doing dressmaking or hat trimming at home, or perhaps baking bread. A few families were left financially provided for, however.

Reading Material (Supplement)

Our folks were great readers. The following media kept us well entertained and informed: *Hillsboro Reflector* and *Hillsboro Mirror,* until they were consolidated and called *The Mirror;* the *Dallas News,* after it started in 1885; the *Courier Journal* of Louisville; the *Southern Cultivator;* the *Youth's Companion; Century Magazine;* and *Iron Age,* of interest to my father in his hardware business. We either had the *Atlanta Constitution* or read Bill Arp, taken from that paper. In later years, we had the *Confederate Veteran, Reviews, Cosmopolitan Magazine,* and *Munsey's.* Among the books were some of Dickens' works, including *Pickwick Papers; Scottish Chiefs;* and, of course, the Bible.

Indicating her interest in culture, my stepmother had busts of Charles Dickens and Beethoven on the top of bookcases in the hall, and a bust of someone else on the piano in the parlor.

Transportation

Most homes were like ours, provided with a saddle horse, or a buggy horse which often served as a saddle horse. The buggy house held a buggy, a surrey, and perhaps a sulky and a gig, and sometimes a buckboard. If one had a sulky, which was a two-wheeled buggy, he might not have any need for a gig, which was more of a racing two-wheeler than a utility sulky. A buckboard was good for light delivery work and hunting. It had no top. One of the first saddles I remember Pa having was a Mexican saddle, with a low horn, with a wide top like a pancake, covered with rawhide. He also had an English or Derby saddle, which we called a muley saddle. Later, we got the standard Texas saddle, and there was at most homes a sidesaddle for the lady. On the farms, of course, was the wagon.

The Clothesline

My memory as to the various details of dress in the decade of 1880 to 1890 is not as well defined as it was in the 1890s and later, though I do recall the main classifications of men's wardrobe.

Most outdoor men, whether farmers or ranchers, preferred the big black hat, which took on various shapes based on the habits of the wearers, and they were often worn until the sweatbands were encrusted and the brim showed plenty of soil. Some of the cowboy hats had the front of the wide brim standing vertical. I can't recall just how the hat managed to stay that way.

My father and other businessmen usually wore a fedora or a derby. The derby became a most popular hat during the 1890s. I can remember having a visit from my father when I was sick, in Winchester, Tennessee, about the year 1890. He wore a little gray derby which was regarded as the latest style. He was one of the best-dressed men in our town. One derby he had had a high crown, and almost approached a top hat in shape, though rounded instead of square top.

Many professional men, such as lawyers and doctors, wore high top hats and Prince Albert coats of black broadcloth.

Pa, and many other businessmen, preferred the frock coat with pockets not only inside, but in the tail. His best suits were usually tailor made.

Boots of various styles were worn a great deal by farmers as well as cowmen and some town people. The farmer's boot had a broad shape and flat heel, suited to walking and to protection of the feet and legs in muddy or wet weather. The cowmen, of course, usually wore the high-heel boots with pointed toes, good enough for the saddle, but poor walking shoes. The horsemen nearly always wore spurs (which the movie men today must not know about). The standard shoe was buttoned on the side. A Congress shoe was convenient to slip on.

The standard shirt was a hard-bosomed white one (or soft cotton or wool work shirts) with detachable collar and tie. When working, men left off these extras, but, when ready to dress up, put them on. Pants were supported by suspenders always, another habit movie writers ignore.

Nearly every man wore a vest, in the pocket of which he carried the "makings," pocket change, and pencils.

The underwear was a shirt and drawers, either tied at the bottom, or elastic.

The Ladies

I have not the temerity nor the professional knowledge to describe the wardrobe of the ladies except in a general way. The clothes of the better-dressed women were made by dressmakers, and their hats trimmed by milliners. Long skirts covered a number of petticoats, chemise, plain or ruffled drawers. Bustles were the usual thing. Instead of trying to have a figure like a young boy, the hips were made to accentuate the hourglass figure. But they looked good to me. Stockings were black lisle or silk, and shoes were buttoned.

Weather Protection

The long, Fish brand, yellow, gummed slicker was the most dependable protection against heavy rain and was usually tied to the back of the saddle when one was out long at a time. Later, a mackintosh was a popular overcoat, having a cape and being water resistant. A well-dressed man, of course, had a nice overcoat.

The pictures that I see hanging in the hall of memory are now to be shown:

A Routine Weekday

Daybreak usually found us all up and doing something. We knew when the neighbors were up by seeing the smoke curling out the kitchen chimney (or "chimbly") and heard the coffee grinder going. The rooster's crow and the calf bawling for his breakfast kept the whole household from oversleeping.

Breakfast found every member of the family at the table before grace was said. And, none of us boys had to be coaxed to eat. One day steak might be served, with eggs, oatmeal, milk toast, butter and preserves. On other days, we might have liver or bacon, with the usual side dishes. No breakfast was to be considered without biscuits and ribbon cane molasses.

After breakfast, we usually had to hurry to finish any chores that had not been attended to before breakfast, such as bringing in plenty of wood and kindling, feeding the chickens, the horse, the cow, and the hogs, and filling the water bucket. Then, we all rushed off to school.

Dinner was not the evening meal, but the noon meal, which most people considered the main meal of the day, for people should not eat too heavy a supper. Dinner could be soup (vegetable usually), roast beef, fish or chicken, plus two or three garden vegetables during the season that could be grown in our garden, such as turnips, greens, beans, peas, okra, and onions. This was followed by pie or peach cobbler. Milk was for children, except in summer ice tea was popular. Coffee was for grown people.

After dinner we would rush back to school. Pa would take a short nap when he could, and then go back to the store.

After school, there were chores to do again, and the cow to milk, and when time allowed, we played stick horse riding, ran races, wrestled, or worked on the bar.

Like all other meals, every member of the family was seated for supper at one time and grace was said. Supper fare would vary. Sometimes it would be patterned a good deal after the dinner menu, but Pa thought children had better not eat meat at night, but something lighter; no one went hungry from the table.

A summer evening usually meant a drive in the surrey, with the grey-lined top and fringe; then, after the sun went down, we would sit on the south front gallery, and talk on any topic, while we watched the lightning bugs blinking in front of us. Pa would tell of his early days in Texas, at the close of the war.

On a winter evening, we would study our lessons for awhile, then sit around the fireplace in the front bedroom and maybe pop popcorn or roast a sweet potato in the ashes. Pa might read to us from the Bible or Bill Arp, in the *Atlanta Constitution*, or I would read the *Youth's Companion*.

When Company Came

That was when the green shutters on the parlor windows were thrown open in the daytime, or closed at night, and if it was winter, a big fire roared in the grate. The "chimbly" in the big hanging lamp was polished with newspapers, and the big family Bible, the photograph album, and the stereopticon pictures were arranged for convenient showing on the marble-topped table. Sometimes everybody sat and talked of times past, and things to come. Sometimes the grown folks would play euchre, or whist, and the children would play authors or checkers. I gave special attention to any visiting ex-Confederate soldier, as we all lived the war over.

Thanksgiving and Christmas

The amount of food one little belly could hold on Thanksgiving and Christmas was almost beyond belief. Turkey, dressing, every kind of good thing, including ambrosia and cake and an orange, were things a kid could dream about long before it happened. Usually, Pa would read aloud Dickens' story of Scrooge. And the thrill of seeing the stockings hanging near the fireplace, with a drum or a wagon on the floor below them, and firecrackers, oranges, candy, roman candles and rockets sticking out of the tops of the stockings, was worth waiting a year for. Oh, yes, and of course, a cap pistol. We did not have firecrackers on the Fourth of July, but they turned us loose on Christmas from before day until bedtime.

July Fourth

That was the day for the big picnic at Abbott's Grove, down Hackberry Creek. The big parade was headed by the brass band, followed by the uniformed firemen, who had charge of the ceremonies on the grounds, followed by a line of Confederate veterans, then buggies, carriages and wagons, or horsemen. We boys would climb trees, run races and eat the big picnic dinner, then hear the town orators of the glories of the Confederacy and add a proper measure for the Founding Fathers.

There would be foot races by the young men, usually running in their sock feet across the grass pasture. And a sack race that gave everybody a laugh.

Adult and Teen-Age Social Customs

Due to the author's concentration of the period on children's activities, the description of the social pleasures enjoyed by teen-agers and active adults has been neglected. The following account of remembered customs will depict the ways for enjoyment of such classes, especially in the Gay Nineties.

As in every age, dancing and card playing was very popular with all young people, though the authorities in the Methodist and Baptist churches frowned on these customs. However, there was no ban enforced, and the lines were often crossed. The most zealous church workers, however, deemed it wrong to participate for fear it might weaken their influence, or make people doubt their sincerity. So, dominoes, Forty-Two, tennis, croquet, buggy riding, bike riding and work in the Epworth League and in the Y.M.C.A. furnished outlets for their desires for social contacts and activities.

As early as I can remember, the Fireman's Annual Ball was a big social occasion. The race track at the fairgrounds, and the nearby Katy Lake, were enjoyed.

Bicycle riding and racing were very popular, as the high-wheeled bicycle gave way to "Safety," which was improved from year to year. Boys and girls got great pleasure out of riding and amateur racing on cow pasture tracks and professional races on dirt tracks, or wooden tracks, were quite exciting. Our town offered one professional, Henry Kirksey.

Electric Streetcars in Hillsboro

I remember well when a streetcar service was installed in Hillsboro, but, because I was away from that town a great deal during that period, and dropping in on vacation periods, I had been unable to pinpoint the dates. I corresponded with everyone in Hillsboro, in my research, including the Electric Light Company, and the Dallas Power and Light Company, without results.

But, in digging through our family archives, which cover a century of family and Hillsboro history, I found a clipping out of a paper, which I am sure must have been the *Hillsboro Mirror* of October 11, 1935, according to a pencil memo written by my father. The following gives a detailed account of the car line's history. I remember the route list he described.

STREETCARS IN HILLSBORO

But that was forty years ago and they only ran for three years and did not prove profitable.

But they were electrically driven

And covered considerable territory, though only one line of track was used.

A good Bynum friend was in last week and asked us when there were streetcars in Hillsboro and whether they were electric driven or mule drawn. We answered that was a good many years before we came to Hillsboro and we did not know but were of the opinion they were mule drawn. We promised to find out.

Various people gave their opinions but none were sure, until we ran across the man who hauled the cars out to the barn from the depot when they came in and back when the line was dismantled. He promised to whip us if we used his name, so we will refrain. But he was in the transfer business in those days and is still one of our best citizens.

He told us of the proper dates. The road came in 1895 and proving unprofitable went out in 1898. It was electric driven, used only one track, but this covered a large section of east Hillsboro, starting at the Katy tracks, running up Elm street to Church, thence north on Church to Franklin, east on Franklin to Corporation, south on Corporation to Second (now Park Drive) and east on Park Drive to an old dog racing track about where the J. G. Weatherby home now stands. The barns were located out at the east end of the track, while the power house was about where the Texas Power and Light Company maintenance office is located near the Katy tracks.

The First Telephone in Hillsboro

The first telephone installed in Hillsboro was on the wall just outside my father's office, in his hardware store on Elm Street, and my brother, Lamar, was then about fourteen years old, in the year 1887, give or take a few months. The calendar date given is based upon the fact that I remember that Lamar was fourteen years old then, and he was born on the nineteenth day of January, the same day and month when we celebrated the general's birthday.

As there were no other local telephones, his only contact was with nearby Milford, Texas, about sixteen miles northeast of town, and Waco, I believe, was the only other outside connection.

My impression is that perhaps Milford had a connection with Dallas, and messages could be relayed, but I have no proof of that.

My brother had a good laugh when a German boot maker ordered some boot leather over the telephone from a Waco store, and the man at the other end of the line had difficulty understanding his pronouncing the word *boot*.

Churches

The First Methodist Church (First Methodist Episcopal

Church South, I think, was the full name) was located on the corner of Waco and Walnut streets. It was a plain little white frame church with a bell tower. Inside was the pastor's study, choir loft and main sanctuary.

Later, a more attractive and larger building was built. My father was a trustee and steward in both churches. My wife and I were married in that second church, in October 1908.

Still later, a very handsome and up-to-date building was erected on Elm Street, which is still serving the congregation. It is well equipped for most any church need.

The other churches in the town, at an early date, as I remember them, were the Baptist, Presbyterian, Cumberland Presbyterian and Episcopalian. Churches were then not serving as places of entertainment, where people ate, danced, played cards and engaged in athletics. They were used exclusively for religious worship.

Sundays were spent quietly, remembering the Bible story of creation, wherein the Lord directed that the seventh day be a day of rest for man and beast. By nine o'clock the church bells all over town announced the opening of Sunday school.

After the superintendent called for order and a song was sung, the secretary was called to the front to read the minutes of the previous Sunday; then the pupils would gather in their respective corners with the teachers for the study of the lesson.

After Sunday school was dismissed and we had a big Sunday dinner, we would read, or take naps and talk. Pa would often read to us. No boisterous playing or such would be permitted. Perhaps a quiet drive in the country would be taken by the family, if the weather was favorable. Sometimes we went to church at night, but not always.

School History

Before beginning my recital of many instances in my lifetime as a pupil in the Hillsboro schools, I wish to call attention to the fact that instead of the trivia reported by me, one can find in his library a *History of the Schools of*

Hillsboro, by my father, J. R. Thompson, Sr. Here he will find a real history, written by one who was a trustee of the Hillsboro School District when it was founded, and one who spent days and nights in scholarly research in the preparation of this excellent book. My father was eminently qualified for this task because he was part of the system from its inception, and was a leader in every department of society through all the following years, so that he kept in touch with affairs; and having had six children attend the public and some private schools in the town, he had a firm base by which diligent study and research were supported.

This book was written in the year 1936, when he was eighty-seven years old, about a year before his death.

Schooling During the 1880s

As stated before, the first schools were small private schools, giving attention to the most elementary studies, and attended usually by younger children. Friday "Evening" called for recitations as a relief from the usual study work. "The Boy on the Burning Deck," was a good starter.

Later, when the Hillsboro Independent School opened, with Professor Coleman and his wife, the list of studies included McGuffy's Readers, beginning with the First Reader, for primary children, and running through the Sixth Reader. Instead of a graded system, the number of the reader indicated the approximate advancement of the student. Of course, arithmetic, spelling, geography, grammar and history were standard diet.

At recess, we played marbles and top spinning in season, ran races, played fox and geese and whip cracker, and baseball. One lively caper was for the small boys to "bump" some of the bigger ones. They would swarm all around and over him until somebody got his leg pulled out from under him so as to get him on the ground. Then a bunch would take hold of his hands and wrists and another bunch would take his feet and raise him up as high as they could, then let him down, stern first, for about three or four good bumps, then let him up.

The Older Boys Go to Bingham Military School in Mebane and Asheville, North Carolina

The year I went to Winchester, my brother, Rodgers, was sent to Bingham Military School, in Mebane, North Carolina. The other brother had planned to go to the Moreland Military Academy in Atlanta, which had been named for a maternal uncle, but "Slow Fever" laid him low for some time, so that his college work did not begin until the next year, when he, Lamar, accompanied Rodgers back to Bingham. But due to a big fire at the school, it was moved to Asheville, North Carolina. Two other Hillsboro boys, Nelson Phillips, later chief justice of the Supreme Court of Texas, and Tom Stroud, attended the school at the same time. Tom Stroud afterward went to West Point, but did not finish.

The school was celebrated as a preparatory school, and as Major Bingham's ambition was to prepare his boys for West Point, he invoked strict military discipline. The major's son, Robert Bingham, was then attending Princeton and Prof. Woodrow Wilson taught history and economics. Robert Bingham ran the school for awhile after his father's death, but later married a Kentucky lady, and became publisher of the *Courier Journal* and, later, ambassador to the Court of St. James.

In the summer of 1931, my wife and I were vacationing in Asheville and visited the site of the old school which had been closed since 1927, after having been operated by one family for about 107 years. It brought back memories to me of the two handsome, healthy-looking, soldierlike brothers who came home that last summer they were there.

Our schooling was partly at public schools, and partly at private schools, including Patterson Institute and Professor Pettitt's school. He was very thorough, but very strict, and was getting along in years with somewhat failing vision.

As the Decade Closes

The decade between 1880 and 1890 was marked by a rapid expansion of railroads over Texas, and a continuing immigration of people from Tennessee, Georgia, Alabama, Arkansas, Mississippi and Louisiana. About that time the Cotton Belt extended a forty-mile tap from its main line at Corsicana to Hillsboro. The M.K.&T. connected Dallas with its main line at Hillsboro, and the Fort Worth and Denver nosed its way across the plains, and other mileage was added in various parts of the state.

At the same time, Scottish and British investors invaded Texas with money to buy land, and money to lend on farms and ranches. In the year 1889, there were about one dozen such companies chartered by the state, a list of which is given in my "Evolution of the Land Mortgage."

All of this created an activity and a development in every little and big town on the railroads, which began to bear fruit during the following decade, despite an economic depression over the land. A wheat boom developed in what we called the Pan Handle, but which area lay southeast of the physical Panhandle; the area referred to was from Wichita Falls west, along the Fort Worth and Denver. Prices for awhile were good and crops abundant, but the 1891 crop was the end of the boom. But it had filled the roads with new buggies and new wagons; the new binders were gathering the crops.

A part of one school year, I was sent to Itasca, a small town twelve miles north of Hillsboro, to work in my father's branch hardware store, which was being managed by a friend, Doc Hatcher. Part of my time was spent in putting up and blacking stoves, and part of it as apprentice to the tinner, which job I had at one time at the Hillsboro store.

The nine-thirty opening hours now in vogue did not apply to us, as one of us had to get to the store about seven o'clock or earlier, open up and sweep out, if it was not done the afternoon before, and then went to breakfast when another clerk who had already had breakfast came to relieve the first one. I gave no great promise as a future merchant, and now realize that I neglected one part of my education by not taking a greater and more curious interest in that type of work. But, as I planned to be a lawyer, why waste time weighing up nails and blacking cookstoves and selling "bob wire"?

Lamar and I Enter Southwestern University, Georgetown, Texas

In the autumn of 1892, my older brother Lamar and I were sent to school at Southwestern University at Georgetown, while my brother Rodgers worked in the store at Hillsboro for awhile. Later, he joined us for a part of the session. He was the mathematician of the family, having inherited that gift from our father. As an example, he afterwards attended a celebrated business college, Eastman Business College, in Poughkeepsie, New York, and made a grade of one hundred from the first day through the final examination, a record that had not been equalled for twenty-five years. A man named Judson, a son of one of Rodgers Bingham schoolmates, repeated these grades twenty-five years later.

Though my brothers spent only a short time at Southwestern University, I started in the Preparatory Department and went through to graduate in June 1898, after staying out one year, from the summer of 1896 to the fall of 1897. As I was not sure of ever getting back to college after that year, and being anxious to graduate with my classmates, I induced the faculty to let me take a double course and by their indulgence did get a diploma the following June.

As the conditions of college life were then so different from those of later years and as they present an interesting and unique contribution to the future of life of so many boys and girls, I deem it desirable to devote a good deal of time to describing the conditions in the late 1890s. My chief inspiration, coupled with the example of my father, sprang from the years I spent in that historic institution. The lives of such men as Dr. Robert S. Hyer, Dr. C. C. Cody, Dr. Allen, Professor Young, as well as the first "regent" when I began school there, Prof. J. H. McLean, meant much in forming my philosophy and religious thought of the later years.

The Southwestern University I attended, beginning in the autumn of 1892 and ending in June 1898, after one year out of school, was very different from the well-equipped, modern school, with a big staff of teachers and ample facilities, but the aura emanating from that old school is still a part of my memory and was an important factor in forming the ideas and ideals that have governed me since then.

My first year and part of the second were spent in the Preparatory Department, as I was only fourteen years old when I entered the school. It was quite a journey to go from Hillsboro to Georgetown, a distance of about one hundred miles. We would board the M.K.&T. southbound train and ride to Taylor, reaching there for dinner at noon, and then catch the main line of the I.&G.N. for Roundrock for early supper, where we would change cars to ride the Georgetown Tap, the remaining ten miles to Georgetown, as the main line ran on to Austin and San Antonio. The M.K.&T. (Katy) went to Houston, and did not then go to Austin or San Antonio.

The first night was spent in the firetrap of a frame hotel, which was later operated by two elderly ladies, on American Plan. Their food was so good that it was a favorite of the traveling man.

The next day, Pa took us around to investigate the available boardinghouses, and left us at Mrs. Saffold's, a fine, motherly, 230-pound lady, who served us an abundance of good wholesome food, and gave us a room for fourteen dollars a month. The house was one room deep, and had a porch running the length of it along the front and back. It was across the street from the college, so that we could sometimes wait until the bell began ringing for chapel service, then bound over the style and to the low one-story chapel in time for roll call. Roll call was done by sections. Each monitor responded for his group.

After a short chapel service, with the regent (now called president) or some member of the faculty leading, we would go to our classes.

The location of Southwestern University up to the last

of the nineteenth century was at the present location of a high school. The foundation for the new administration building, several blocks east of this location, was started in the spring of 1898, the year I graduated. The building was probably finished not long afterward. I went back about two or three years later, in the spring of 1901, to take a commercial course and some advanced English, and the school had been moved.

The Main Building and School Activities

Here is a description of the plant that served us during the 1890s. The main school building was a rock-ribbed three-story square building, with wide halls running through the center and three recitation rooms on each side. A bell tower crowned it. In the southeast corner, downstairs, was Dr. Robert Stuart Hyer's recitation room, and adjoining it was a small laboratory. On the third floor, the northeast corner room was set aside for the San Jacinto Literary Society, and the northwest corner room for the Alamo Society. These two bodies formed the center of social and political life of the school on a broad basis among the boys. Greek letter fraternities naturally represented a segment of society, but the political fortunes of Barbs and Frats was determined in the halls of these two societies. Near the end of my undergraduate days a new society, called the Henry W. Grady, was organized and occupied another third-floor room.

We had a bad case of oratory in those days. There would be declamation contests for the preps, and each society would choose three boys to compete before the faculty at some later date. I tried my hand as one of the three from the San Jacinto Society, but I was "often a bridesmaid, but never a bride" in the many contests from prep to senior. The close call came when, in our sophomore year, we had an oratorical contest and Clyde Sweeton and I got two each of the five votes of the judges, but on later ballot, he got the deciding vote. He afterwards became a prominent member of the firm of Vinson, Elkins, Sweeton and Weems, a large Houston law firm.

In addition to contests for medals in every category, from prep and freshman declarations (recitals of memorized classics), through sophomore, junior and senior class contests, there was a contest before the faculty to determine who should represent the school in a statewide intercollegiate contest. This grew out of an organization which the late Bishop Hiram A. Boaz promoted, called the State Oratorical Association.

Our representatives were selected according to custom, by each Literary Society electing three men to compete before the faculty committee. The winner then went to the state contest. Mr. Boaz, who afterward became vice-president, then president of Southern Methodist University, and later, Bishop, was our first representative at the state contest, and he won the first gold medal.

Among the colleges competing were A&M, Trinity University, Austin College, and Baylor University, as I remember them. Texas University deemed it undesirable to join, for fear, I take it, that their status would be lowered. At that time Morris Shepherd, afterward U.S. senator, was the fair-haired orator of State University. We were anxious to try our mettle on him but were not allowed to. In afteryears, Southwestern won several medals, one of them at Sherman, when my father, J. R. Thompson, Sr. of Hillsboro, Judge Head of Sherman, and Tom Smith of Hillsboro, were the judges. Smith was either then Speaker of the House of Representatives or attorney general, I have forgotten, as he held both offices during my school days.

The contest that generated more fervor than any other, however, was the Commencement Debate, held at the closing days of the school session. Each society selected two debaters, and they had to be good, to debate some question of public interest, such as the federal pensions, at a time when the people of the South could not put their hands in this flesh pot, as only a few of the residents then were ex-soldiers of the Union army. If a tape recording of these speeches could have been kept, it would reveal a thoroughness in study of the questions at issue that might astonish us today. A member of Congress, in addressing us one day, stated that he had never heard such exhaustive and thorough presentation of a subject in the U.S. Senate as these boys offered that night. Every magazine published was studied diligently for weeks before the time.

Among the winners that I remember in the original oratorical college contests were Hiram A. Boaz, Beal Sneed (or Snead), Knox Porter, and McQuire, and the last one I remember was my very dear friend, John E. Green, Jr., who in later years became general attorney for the Gulf Oil Company in Houston. He graduated the year I took my special commercial course.

More About the Buildings

Back to the description of the buildings that housed our boys and that are now etched on my brain: In the southwest corner of the campus was a one-story chapel building of white limestone, where chapel services were held each morning before we went to classes and where the commencement exercises were held, and where celebrated lecturers, such as Bob Taylor, Eli Perkins, and others entertained us at times. These men were invited by our lecture committee and gave us most of the outside entertainment we enjoyed. In addition to lectures, we heard the Swiss Bell Ringers, the Schubert Quartet, and others.

In the Halls of Learning

I now seek to present brief word pictures of the members of the Southwestern University faculty who were serving in the closing decade of the nineteenth century, when I enjoyed my prep and college years.

Dr. John H. McLean, Regent

A tall bearded man, a Methodist minister with strong moral convictions, he demanded correct conduct by all people connected with the university. He earned the respect of everyone who knew him. He taught one or more senior subjects. I attended none of his classes, as he retired right after my sophomore year.

Dr. Robert Stewart Hyer, Science Professor

Dr. Hyer, a man of outstanding mental and moral stature, was a scientist highly rated among his peers. He was a scholarly man. Though his dignified mien might cause some to think he was an egoist, he was a very modest person. In addition to his work in the laboratory and in the classroom, he brought the first X-ray to the South and operated it. After Dr. McLean's retirement, he served as chairman of the faculty, and afterwards as regent, and president. Later, he became president of Southern Methodist University when it was founded. He was a thorough Bible student and teacher.

Dr. Claude C. Cody, Math Professor

Dr. Cody was a tall, slender man, with a slight stoop. He was a man of strong moral character, a courteous gentleman in the classroom or in social life. He was a welcome guest in one's home, by his modest and quiet manners. In addition to his duties as mathematics teacher, he managed the Mood Hall, a combination dormitory and mess hall.

Dr. Vaden, Professor of Greek and Latin

Dr. Vaden was a man of medium stature, and a lover of music, and, I believe, of some talent. He seemed to enjoy pacing in front of the class when he scanned the first lines of Virgil. I did not know him intimately, but regarded him as a scholarly gentleman of quiet manners. He married a charming Georgetown lady while I was in school.

Dr. Young, Professor of German and Spanish

Dr. Young (known as "Brigham"), was a solid man of

quiet manners and deliberate speech. I cherish one of the last words I remember his speaking to me. Our senior examination papers were in the hands of the faculty members, and I knew I had made poor grades, after trying to cover two years in one; so, when meeting Dr. Young on the campus, I boldly asked him, "Dr. Young, have you had time to examine my grades yet?"

"Yes, you passed."

'Nuf said. My companion got a good laugh at my performance.

Dr. H. A. Shands, Professor of English

Dr. Shands was a good-looking young blond with a freshly inked Ph.D. degree tucked away which had been granted by the University of Mississippi. He was a cultivated man who had some misgivings on his first visit to our class, as he did not know just how rough those Texas cowboys might be, but he soon learned that we were not so bad, and he enjoyed the work. He, too, won the affections of a charming Georgetown lady, and they were married.

Dr. John R. Allen, Professor of Philosophy and Logic

Dr. Allen was director of the Ladies Annex, a building on a separate campus, about a half mile from the main building, which served as dormitory, dining room and classrooms for the out-of-town girls. Some of the young ladies in senior classes came to the main campus for instruction.

He was a short, plump man with poor vision, who took seriously the responsibility for the care of his young lady students, with the aid of Mrs. Allen and a matron. On one occasion when some boys invaded the Annex campus to serenade the girls without receiving permission, they decided to retreat when the good doctor appeared with a double-barrel shotgun and let fly on the fleet-footed musicians.

Frank Dobie admired Dr. Allen very much, as he attended the university for a while.

Professor Mowry, Commercial Department

Professor Mowry was perhaps five feet ten or eleven, well proportioned, and a quiet, industrious man who taught bookkeeping and shorthand. Three years after graduating, I took a few months' course in his department, and advanced English under another professor.

Dr. Moore, Principal of Preparatory Department

Dr. Moore was a tall man with a mustache, and because of his deliberate movements I suppose, was dubbed "Sleepy Moore," even after he became professor in Southern Methodist University. I had moved into college as a freshman when Dr. Moore came to S.W.U., so did not have frequent contacts with him, but the fact that he became a professor of English at S.M.U. indicates that he was a man of ability.

Dr. Pegues

Dr. Pegues was another professor in the prep department when I was in school, and he too became a member of the S.M.U. faculty. I did not know him very well. He appeared to me as being about six feet tall and well proportioned. He married a lovely Georgetown lady.

Dr. Fontane

I think Dr. Fontane was the name of the young man who was teaching in the Preparatory Department when I entered the school in the fall of 1892. He was a slender, good-looking young man who was very thorough in his work. A photograph of the faculty members, in my file, shows the picture of a young man, who I think was Dr. Carroll.

We respected each member of the university faculty, as we believed they were sincere men of ability and good-will. Southwestern University was like a big family, from which I did not take much dollar value learning, but where the moral code which I had been taught to respect at home was continued.

Fire Fighters

Fire fighters are now and have all my life been an important group in our society. The work of the firemen, however, is today very different from that in the last two decades of the nineteenth century, and their equipment of today is so superior to the tools of those men of that early day, it may be of interest to review the history of activities of these important institutions.

The most exciting thing that ever happened to the small boys of the 1880s was to be awakened in the dead of night by the sound of the fast clanging of the fire bell and the pistol and gun shots telling us of a fire. Everybody got dressed as quickly as possible, so as to miss none of the thrill of watching excited people rush around and drag stuff from the burning building as long as they could, while the firemen grabbed hold of the long rope handholds as well as the tongue of the hook-and-ladder truck or the fire engine, and pulled the equipment to the burning structure. On one occasion, a cowboy, Jack Leary, (or Lerry) rode up, and tied a rope to the end of the line, then to his saddle horn, which helped the men a great deal.

If the fire was in the business section, which meant on the Courthouse Square or a block or two from it, the water source was two big underground cisterns, one on the east side of the square, and other on the west.

The hook-and-ladder truck usually got to the fire first. while the fire engine was warming up. Underneath the truck there hung a long row of rubber buckets which were filled, and a human chain formed to carry the water to the building and wet as much as could be reached. This was often the only means of fighting the fires of burning homes, where the water had to come from pumps in the yards. Naturally, every able-bodied man, whether fireman or not, could help form the human chain.

Piles of furniture or merchandise were often stacked in the street before the flames got too strong. When my father's hardware store caught fire, years later, a great effort was made to first get out the powder cans and the loaded ammunition shells to reduce the explosions. For safety, however, most of the black powder of that day was kept outside the city limits in a brick "Powder House."

Pete Mitenthall, owner of a combination grocery store and beer distributor, opened a keg of beer to aid the brave fighters. After a store burned, the merchant always sent a check to the fire boys.

A few years later, big draft horses pulled the equipment, including the engines and fire truck, but maybe the hose carts would be pulled by the boys. And, at the annual conventions of the Volunteer Firemen, there would be races of about fifty to one hundred yards to connect with the nearest plug (city water then being available) and start the water. Teams would run against time.

In my city town hall is a long row of portraits arranged along the wall, showing the faces of fire chiefs over the years. Among them are many faces of men who later became leading citizens of the town, and of the state or nation. One, Melvin A. Traylor, became president of the First National Bank of Chicago, and of the American Bankers Association, and a power in financial circles.

The Volunteer Firemen became an active political segment of the local community and one state official got a big help from the cadres formed in each small town over the state. In course of time, the motorized equipment improved the effectiveness of the firemen's work.

Dallas in 1886

The night sky was turning to pearl gray that morning as Grandpa Johnston and I stood on the lonely platform of the M.K.&T. Railroad station. I was soon to live a dream that had long been cherished and nursed in my young mind. I was going to visit Uncle Alex White and Aunt Norry and, especially, Cousin Abby, in Dallas. My older brothers had told me of the charm of that home. They would stay at home to look after the livestock and other responsibilities while the grown folks were enjoying a vacation near the town of Bentonville, Arkansas.

Grandpa, an ex-Confederate soldier, was starting on his way to revisit his old home in Georgia, and would drop me off at Dallas for my visit.

There was no direct rail line to Dallas in that year 1885 or 1886, as the Dallas branch, which my father helped promote, did not reach us until about 1890. We had to go to Fort Worth where we would catch the Texas and Pacific, eastbound, for Dallas.

On arriving at Dallas, Grandpa rushed me to the waiting Belt Line streetcar, and told the driver to take me to the home of Judge Alex White on Harwood Street. The driver did not know the place but said he would find out on the way.

The Belt Line was a four-mile long line, with little cars drawn by mules. At well-spaced distances there would be a switch, where one car would wait until a car coming from the other direction would pass. The driver would question the other man when he came to the switch and was told to "stop at that big, two-story house on the right, with its 'Aarn' fence around the front yard where there was lots of flowers and shrubs."

I was embarrassed as I got off just before the car had come to a full stop, and sat down in the sand beside the track, but held on to my little, black, imitation alligator valise.

Cousin Abby greeted me warmly, and a life of untroubled pleasure began in that high-ceiling parlor with its white plastered walls and inside Venetian shutters which were raised or lowered just as a window would be. The real luxury, though, was the long zinc tub, with running water, where on a hot summer day I could lie flat and enjoy myself, instead of taking a washtub to the kitchen for my weekly scrub. I enjoyed taking the hose and watering the flowers when it was permitted.

Uncle Alex spent much of his time, when at home, in his well-stocked library. He was a tall, slender man who was always dressed in a Prince Albert coat and high hat.

My father said he had won two damage suits, yielding fees of $10,000 and $15,000, an unheard of amount of money to us. I have letters from him about that time, addressed to my father, giving his office address at 511 Elm Street. On one visit to his office with my father, we went to the top of that four-story skyscraper and took a look over Dallas with its few blocks of rock-paved streets in the business section. Later, many of the streets were to be paved with bois d'arc blocks.

On one visit to Dallas, Cousin Abby took me to Oak Cliff over the new elevated car line. And, on another occasion, I accompanied her to the spot down on the edge of the Trinity River where they had a ladies' bathing place and I waited outside until the ladies, properly dressed for the street, appeared. The population of Dallas then was between twenty thousand and twenty-five thousand. There have been some changes in the last eighty-one years. Selah.

Portraits of a Great Lady and an Orator of Note

This story is taken from an issue of *Alcalde*, a magazine published by the alumni association of The University of Texas, during the 1920s.

WHAT PORTRAITS HAVE YOU IN YOUR MENTAL PICTURE GALLERY?
Gretchen Rochs Goldschmidt, A. '03

Nothing, nothing, not even a hasty look at the mirror, or increasing dentist's bills, gives one as adequate an idea of the passage of time as do the styles of women's "ready to wear." Half an hour ago, a cavalcade of young ladies passed the house — equestriennes from the army post, presumably! They wore — to begin at the pedal extremities — very businesslike boots and leggings, form-fitting britches (spell, breeches), white mannish shirts and black ties. Some were bare-headed, others wore a sort of feminized and modified rough-rider hat. Trim and sporty they appeared, yet immediately my memory which harks back too much, my daughter informs me, to the Nifty 'Nineties, reproduced a series of mental portraits.

And I want you to come with me and see whether you recognize some of those old masterpieces.

Can you see a young lady riding across the capitol grounds? What a picture of grace, skill, beauty and horsemanship! The black close-fitting riding-habit that only a woman of superb physique could carry off to perfection, the shining beaver with its fluttering veil, so picturesque, so unutilitarian, the gauntlets, the riding-crop, the long sweep of the robe over the feet; the erect and of necessity a bit unnatural carriage in the side-saddle, all this is now as extinct as the Dinosaur; still none of those who saw the golden-haired Amazon of that time can forget the stately beauty and the thrill of it.

Ima Hogg, unapproachable as she appeared seen atop the gallant steed, was in reality a charming freshman, unaffected in manner and a most conscientious student. We attended the same classes and often planned to do our lessons together. I can well recall the picture of the cozy library at the Hogg home, where we studied one afternoon; in the next room the ex-governor was entertaining a friend. After a bit, the murmuring voices grew more distinct, and I lost all interest in the books.

"What a voice!" I cried out. "It wraps itself round your heart like a warm flannel rag!" "It ought to be a good voice," Ima replied, amused at my awed levity, "it's made him famous."

"Who is it?" I asked. "Why it's William Jennings Bryan. He always comes to see father when he's in Texas. Would you like to meet him?"

Of course I was delighted. Like all the rest of my time, I had read his famous "Cross of Gold" speech and through the ear-tubes of those fore-runners of the modern talking machine, had heard it coming across the crude contrivance in almost undiminished splendor. Even so, the magic re-sonance of those tones were strangely disturbing. We quickly put away our books and papers and went into the next room. Here my memory serves me with a fine portrait of a genial statesman, then at the zenith of his power. His eyes were good, his mobile mouth and his forehead impressive, but the voice — the voice! Smooth, deep, with a vibrant metallic timbre. He said, "How are you, young ladies?" and it became an event. Before we left, I had the temerity to ask him for an auto-graph and had added an anecdote to the collection of newspaper articles about himself he was mak-ing. (I presume he has long since tired of gather-ing up what the papers are saying about him, and dismal reading it would make nowadays.) The day before I had seen a copy of *Life* and one of the full-page illustrations showed the famous Hogg ostriches, Jack and Jill. Jill was reported asking Jack: "Will you let that man Bryan ride you when he comes to Texas?" "No, ma'am," was the emphatic rejoinder, "he's ridden one hobby to death," referring, of course, to the free silver issue. The great Commoner seemed to enjoy that one hugely. How our heroes shrink in afteryears. If cartoons were allowed in a picture gallery, there would be one of a thin-lipped zealot, fran-tically waving a burned-down torch, blotting out the clear sunlight of Truth with its darkling smoke.

My regret now is that, hypnotized by the cajol-ing voice of Bryan, I failed to get a clear portrait

of the much greater man, perhaps the most prominent Texan of the last fifty years, Governor Hogg.

The Ladies' Annex

A very important building, the Ladies' Annex, was not
located on the main campus, but was on a large campus
area at the eastern edge of the town. This served as dormitory, mess hall and schoolhouse for most of the young
ladies attending Southwestern whose homes were out of
town. Some who were in advanced classes came to the
Main Building for some of their recitations.

This was a very substantial brick structure of about
three or four stories, built in a T shape. The young ladies
wore blue uniforms at all times except on special occasions,
such as those participating in the commencement exercises,
such as musical recitals and essay reading, when they wore
the conventional pretty white dresses, which a mere man
does not know how to describe, though he could admire
them just the same.

This blue line trooped to church service and other
services, dressed in their uniforms, and as Dr. Allen was
a bit nearsighted, some of the boys were able to drop in
the line at night and visit with the girls, but not often,
as a matron rode herd on one end of the line while Dr.
Allen steered the other.

No Panty Raids at Southwestern U. in 1897

There were two reasons for no panty raids at Southwestern U. back in the year 1897; the underpinning worn
by the young ladies was much longer and of much heavier
material. The other reason is that the Reverend John R.
Allen tolerated no nonsense in the operation of the Ladies'
Annex to Southwestern University. He deemed it his duty
to protect the sanctity of the campus and respect for the
young ladies entrusted to the care of the good doctor and
his wife.

The word of a member of the faculty in those days
carried authority, and in addition to the force of his words,

the Reverend John R. Allen had a more convincing weapon whose authority few wanted to dispute.

I was not an eyewitness to the activities of some school boys and Dr. Allen on that chilly spring night, but I have the story from responsible sources. This happened the year I was out of the university, but a full report was made to me on my return in the following fall. I had an amusing but less-exciting experience one foggy night of the following season.

A small group of college boys had been serenading the girls, using all manner of unmusical instruments, such as tin pans, combs, tuneless guitars, and off-key vocal renditions, when the door opened and Dr. Allen appeared on the front porch with a leveled double-barrel shotgun pointing at the then fast-retreating boys. He let fly with one barrel, then the other, but did not slow the pace of the intruders. It is believed that some records were made that night by boys who never entered track contests.

The next day some of the boys, on sick leave, went to Austin, thirty miles away, so that a nonresident doctor could pick a few pellets out of their backsides.

Next year, when we of the San Jacinto Literary Society held open house and had special guests, the ladies of the Annex and Dr. and Mrs. Allen, we entertained them with a stirring debate, as follows: "Resolved that the wounded veterans of Annex Hill, of 1897, should be pensioned."

We stressed the unsportsmanlike conduct of the shotgun wielder in taking a potshot at the boys in this compact group, fleeing for their lives. The rule of all sports was to give the game a chance to escape.

The following autumn, we asked and received Dr. Allen's permission to serenade the girls, but the night we planned it something came up that prevented us; so, one foggy night, while the "Dirty Dozen" were strolling around, we met a few Negro boys with guitars and other instruments and engaged them to furnish the music for us, at a price of a dollar a head. Suddenly one of them stopped and said, "Naw Suh, Naw Suh. I ain't goin' up there and get my head shot off for no dollar." But when I assured him that we had permission to serenade the Annex, he said, "Where is that man who got permission? I am goin' to hang on to him."

We told the musicians to go on up on the front gallery, while we stood back behind some trees in the fog, but they would not go without one of us joining them. Clyde Sweeton went with them, and when the boys started tuning up the matron appeared at the door and said, "No serenading allowed at the Annex without permission. Who are you, anyway?"

"We is niggers," came the answer. Then, she said, "Real Negroes?" and Clyde answered, "Yessum." But when the doors were opened wide she saw him standing there, which called for an explanation. He told of having Dr. Allen's permission, but naturally he knew that Dr. Allen was then in Dallas attending an annual conference of the Methodist church. After Clyde's explanation, she demanded that all of us come to the light, so she would know who was on the campus.

Gay Nineties

There was some foundation for the term *Gay Nineties,* perhaps, since it was a period when people danced and sang many new songs, and there were no war clouds on the horizon until the Spanish-American War started as the sun went down on the nineteenth century.

But to one who lived in the part of America where cotton and cattle meant everything in the way of economic conditions, it seemed more in the nature of a sober, sane, but tight time, for at least the first few years of that decade, as drought was added to the low prices for commodities, thus reducing the income to the minimum for decent living. But it was natural and proper for everyone to be economical which usually levels a population during long periods of depression.

As an example of the value of a dollar during this period, I was told by my brother Lamar, who was in charge of Pa's branch store in the nearby town of Itasca, that if I could sell a box of shaft-supporters and anti-rattlers for $1.50 each, I could pocket half the money. It was really a handy gadget; when the horse walked out of the shafts, a spring would lift them up and there was a rubber contraption where the shaft was hinged that kept them from rattling.

Though I stopped at every farm and ranch house in reach of the road in that twelve-mile drive to Hillsboro, I did not sell a single one. I remember the usual answer: "No, Bud, we can't buy anything like that with four-cent cotton." I did sell one set to a Hillsboro doctor who boarded at the same place we did at that time.

The most impressive monument to the new decade in our hometown was the fine, new, three-story courthouse with its tall clock tower. This handsome building of native white rock took the place of the two-story red brick building which had been there as long as I could remember. This courthouse, just built while my Uncle John D. Abney was county judge, was said to cost one hundred thousand dollars, and to be the finest courthouse in Texas.

In addition to the various offices and vaults, there was a big auditorium on the second floor which had a ceiling above the third floor, and a horseshoe balcony ran around the north, east and west sides of the building, on a level with the third floor, the doors of which provided entrance and exit. Here, folks from all over the county would gather during political campaigns to hear their favorite orators. Here, James Stephen Hogg spoke in his race for governor of Texas, and the voices of such stalwarts as Joseph W. Bailey, Cone Johnson, M. M. Crane, Cullen Thomas, Judge John H. Reagan, Charles Culberson, Pat Neff, and my old college classmate, R. Ewing Thomason, now federal judge in El Paso, thundered, while the palm leaf fans were trying to keep the corseted ladies comfortable. My first sight of this was when I returned from a year at school in Winchester, Tennessee, in the year 1890.

Among the noteworthy happenings of this decade at the sundown of the nineteenth century were the election of Grover Cleveland in 1892 to a second term as president, and the election of William McKinley in 1896, and the

Spanish-American War, which started Teddy Roosevelt on his march to the White House, as he hoped it would. And, the giant, James Stephen Hogg, became governor of Texas and founded the Texas Railroad Commission, which has had the most outstanding record of accomplishment of any bureau in the state, but now giving the principal part of its time to the oil and gas regulation. The Hon. Judge John H. Reagan headed the first Commission.

My father, Joseph Rodgers Thompson, Sr., known to his close friends as "J. R.," was the chairman of the Hill County for Hogg Campaign Committee. In fact, it had by then become a habit for him to be chairman of committees for the betterment of the community, as he had been chairman of the committee which sought the extension of the M.K.&T. Railroad from Dallas to Hillsboro, and the Cotton Belt Railroad from Corsicana. He had headed the chamber of commerce which then bore a different label, and had sent to the Corn Palace at Fort Worth a six-foot column of Hill County black dirt in a glass case, to show the world why Hill County was such a cotton producer.

During this period, my father, who had been managing the Hillsboro Roller Mill, found that there was not enough wheat raised in this nearly all cotton county to make it profitable to operate any longer the mill which had been built by a civic-minded group of people; so he urged them to move it to the wheat country, as the breadbasket of Texas stretched from Denton, through Gainesville, on to Wichita Falls, and up to Fort Worth and Denver, giving Fort Worth first call on the wheat fields.

At an early date, perhaps about 1888, the merchants began taking on city ways. Dunham and Patty, afterwards Patty and Brockington, was on the corner of the east side of the square and the north corner of Elm and the square. This building, in the course of time, was occupied for awhile by Citizens National Bank, and later by Flannagan Bros., a men's clothing store.

The outstanding stores in the way of up-to-date equipment were the pioneers in such matters, the Rosenbaum Bros., store on the east side of the square. They had "Cash" boys running from the salesmen to the cashier to make change. Later the cash boy was replaced with machinery in the form of wire cables on which the cash was shot from the salesman to the cashier and back.

The outstanding dry goods store was the Graham Store, established in 1890, headed by the best-known man who ever lived in Hill County, Charles F. Graham, master salesman. The store was owned by him, his sister, Miss Jessie Graham, and Mr. A. E. Graham (no relation), of Lewisville, and was part of a chain of stores over north and central Texas, one being under the management of Charlie's brother, W. T. Graham, my wife's father, who had a store in Greenville for years, and in Palestine, and later came to Hillsboro and joined the Graham Store there. At one time the Grahams were in Dallas, with great promise, but later got into these smaller towns.

When Charlie Graham hit Hillsboro, he took a year's contract for advertising in the *Hillsboro Mirror*, and was such a hail-fellow-well-met that it would be difficult for anyone to enter that store without his hailing him in a voice and a laugh that could he heard across the street. Afterwards, he and his sons, Will and Fletcher, and daughter, Etta Jess, bought the White House Store in Beaumont, and made large fortunes there. Mr. W. T. in the meantime had retired from the store.

As so much of my description of conditions in our hometown in the middle 1880s showed some primitive and crude living conditions, I may have failed to record the decided change in living conditions during the remainder of the nineteenth century; hence these addenda are to be inserted in the Gay Ninety period.

By the beginning of the last decade of the century, an artesian well, two thousand feet deep, had been drilled and an abundance of artesian water was furnshed the folks in Hillsboro, replacing the many shallow wells of hard, limestone water, which were a menace to health. My father said the incidence of slow fever and such ailments decreased notably after that well was drilled.

Electricity and telephones were installed in many places,

and, believe it or not, we had an electric streetcar line running for a mile or more east from the M.K.&T. depot to the edge of town. This did not last long, and my efforts to learn through the Hillsboro Chamber of Commerce the date of this progressive institution were in vain; no one in Hillsboro seems to know. I think it was during the 1890s.

The mark of business activity and the vitality in the towns along the railroad were recognized by the density of the web of telephone lines across the main street. Hillsboro was a lively place from about 1888 on through the several following years. Later, the wires were put underground.

But we still drove over the dusty streets in long dry spells, and fought the black waxy mud in the wet spells. But brick buildings took the place of the frame buildings in the business section. About the oldest masonry building was the rock saloon, across the alley from Bond's Drugstore on the square.

In the Gay Nineties the young folks never evidenced any signs of the blues, but sang, joked and had their parties. The current songs were popular.

Chuck Wagon Days in the Gay Nineties

The hardworking boys from the farms, stores, railroad yards and the far-flung ranches told their jokes as we lay in the yard on mattresses or tarps.

During harvest and threshing time, the chuck wagon was the center of attraction, three times a day.

The cook and I arose at 4:00 A.M. While he was preparing breakfast, I would feed and water the work stock, and when the cook had breakfast ready, he would beat on the back of a skillet with his butcher knife and yell, "Chuck!" which often failed to get much action, so he yelled in a louder voice. "Chuck, BLANK BLANK!"

Certain items appeared on the tables three times a day: "Java," (or the Local), hot biscuits, fried salt bacon, navy beans, butter, molasses (ribbon cane), and spuds. At dinner and supper, many things were added, such as raw onions, fresh or canned vegetables, stewed tomatoes, corn bread, stewed, dried apples, peaches, apricots (or a cobbler made of such) or pies. Sometimes, fried chicken and blackberries were added to the menu.

The men never went away from the table hungry. One man drank so much coffee that I found a double-sized cup for him, so that he required fewer refills.

Our chuck wagon was unlike the ones so often pictured in trail-driving days, and I think it was much better.

The wagon bed was low, on flat, broad, iron wheels. The kitchen stove, safe and cabinet were at the back end of the wagon. On each side of the wagon, wide plank sides were hinged to the wagon; these were let down, for a table, so that the men, sitting on long low benches, could be served as if at home. A big tarp fastened at the top was stretched out on poles for shelter over the workers. The cook could serve the boys easily from his place in the wagon. Some cooks were good, but now and then one would fail on his biscuits — either half raw, or yellow with soda. All such items were big, about the size of a saucer, and thick.

The cook had time for reading and resting.

Texas' First X-Ray

Southwestern University is a small, church-sponsored school, located in Georgetown, Texas, and presents a very different front in its physical appearance now than did the school back in the middle of the 1890s, but even then, with its crude equipment and small faculty, its science department was the first to bring to the South the new X-ray machine. This was due to the fact that its science professor, Dr. Robert Stewart Hyer, was rated one of the outstanding researchers in the country, despite the fact that his laboratory was in one room adjoining his lecture room. He later became president of Southwestern, and after that, president of Southern Methodist University.

I know of only one other person now living who worked with me helping Dr. Hyer with his early experiments with the new machine — Federal Judge (Retired) R. Ewing Thomason, of El Paso.

On one occasion Dr. Hyer located a needle in a lady's foot while we looked on, and we helped with such muscle work as was needed.

Another time, we located a bullet in a man's back, near his spine. He was paralyzed in his legs, but having been shot once, and having fallen off a telephone pole another time, the doctors did not seem to know the cause of his crippled condition. I did not learn what happened to him after we made the picture, but suppose he had an operation.

The court at Waco refused to admit Dr. Hyer's picture of a man's shoulder in a lawsuit in which he claimed it was broken. The picture was clear enough, but it was ruled inadmissible in evidence.

It is a wonder that we did not get in bad shape by our careless projecting with the machine when alone in the laboratory — taking the pictures of each other's skeletons without any of the precautions now demanded. We did not develop any pictures, but just looked at each other's skeletons.

At the same time, Dr. Hyer was working night after night on experiments for wireless telegraphy, and did send a message from the college to the Williamson County Courthouse about a mile away. He told me that he thought he would beat the world to the discovery because he would persevere longer, but later, Marconi beat him to it. When I next saw him, he said, "Yes, he stumbled on it first."

Dr. Hyer was not only a recognized scientist, but one of the most accurate men in the use of correct English that I ever knew and a man of such strong Christian character that he was respected by everyone who knew him.

The Magic of Miss Annie Abbott

The story you are about to read is true. The names are not changed, because none of the actors now live to challenge my statements, as the drama was enacted in the twilight of another century. But, would one witness appear, he would affirm and perhaps embellish my story.

The student body of Southwestern University each year selected a "Lecture Committee," to bring a number of entertainers to the school, including speakers, musical performers, or other folks for the enjoyment of a church-sponsored school. Gov. Bob Taylor of Tennessee, his brother Alf, Ely Perkins, Gen. John B. Gordon, Swiss Bell Ringers, and others appeared from time to time.

But a slender, one-hundred-pound lady put on a show that puzzled the wise ones more than Pharaoh's dreams did his soothsayers.

She asked that about ten or a dozen prominent citizens be selected to test her magic powers, the source of which she herself did not understand.

She stood on one foot and held a broomstick in her hands and challenged three men to push her off balance. One man would grasp the stick and push, and two other men would push on the shoulder of the man in front of him, without budging the little lady.

Her next stunt was to place an egg between each hand and the wall, and let the man try to break the eggs. No soap.

Then, she selected one of our seniors named Milam, a giant of a man, not less than about six feet, five inches, and after placing her finger on his neck, under the collar, she asked him to lift her. He would appear to strain but could not get her off the ground. Then, removing her finger, she would say, "Why, I weigh only one hundred pounds. You should be able to lift me," and up she would come.

By pointing to someone sitting in the audience, she would dictate whether or not he could stand. The other astonishing things done have escaped my memory, but they were all equally astonishing.

Among the men on the stage were three or four members of the college faculty, some prominent students, and some business and professional men from the town of Georgetown. None of these could offer any explanation except our science professor, Dr. Robert S. Hyer, who said he did not want to claim that the lady's power was anything but astonishing, but he felt sure that she had so hypnotized each one so that the contrary muscles offset the pushing muscles so that there was no real force brought against her. As a proof, he later worked some similar controls over other subjects. So help me, all I have written is true.

Ancient Institutions and Customs that Crossed the Century Line

Any chronicle that omitted Bond's Drugstore from its description of Hillsboro, past and present, would be lacking in completeness.

Dr. William Bond, a stout, kindly gentleman, had his drugstore on the south side of the Courthouse Square as far back as I can remember. He had a custom of giving every little boy who came into the store a little square of chewing gum, with the salutation, "Bud, would you like a chew of wax?" And no one declined. If a kid was sent to a drugstore after a bottle of castor oil, it was not hard to guess which store he would go to. As Dr. Bond lived almost back of the store and kept such long hours, few people ever saw him on the street. In fact, a tale was made up that about ten years after the new courthouse was built, he stood in his front door and said, "I'll declare, I did not know we had such a fine courthouse." He was loved by one and all. And, to add to the popularity of the store he installed a soda water fountain at an early date.

In the course of time, Bond's Alley became quite an institution as the old white-whiskered, retired men would gather in the alley between the store and the adjoining building and swap yarns and spit tobacco all day long. Even though my father lived to be nearly eighty-eight years old, he never joined that fraternity, as he preferred to go to his little office in the Brin Building in his later years, where he could do much writing and see his friends and answer the telephone.

Among the time-honored customs, there were some that

were still observed when I left my hometown in 1923. First Monday and Saturday evenin' are described next.

Other Institutions and Customs

Mr. George Owens, vice-president of Republic National Bank of Dallas, once said that the only laws which were recognized in the part of East Texas from which he came were "Ten Commandments and Ten Percent." I think the ten percent was of a more fixed nature than the Ten Commandments in their observance.

There were other customs always observed in the cotton belt of Central Texas, and perhaps in East Texas, that were just about as changeless as the laws of the Medes and Persians, such as:

Monday was wash day, and if you did not see the clothes on the line you would know it was not Monday, for the old black wash pot on the fire in the yard, with the yellow laundry soap and starch ready, was a regular Monday morning chore.

Saturday Evenin' was set aside for the cotton farmer to go to town whether or not he had any business there. If it rained most of the week, so that he could not get in the field until Thursday or Friday, the plows, cultivators, and hoe hands stopped work at dinner time, so that the man of the house could go to town, and usually the rest of the family went too, though that was not mandatory.

The real estate offices, the drugstore and the barbershops offered comfortable harbors, or now and then some could roost on the iron rail which protected a passage from the street to a basement. I made a sale of a fine home in Hillsboro, during the depression of 1921, to one of my well-to-do farmer friends from Whitney, as we sat on this roost and talked of this and that. I said, "Charlie, are you not ready to move to town? If so, you can get a bargain," etc. etc.

First Monday was an institution that started a long time ago. It originally was for the purpose of selling at auction such stray stock as had been held unclaimed for the period legally provided for, and the first Monday in each month was the day they were to be offered for sale, and was known as *Stray-Sales Day*, but most people called it First Monday. This, too, was a time long hallowed by tradition for the farmers to go to town, and maybe swap horses, cows, mules, or buy something, or just swap conversation.

For twelve months, or more, the local chamber of commerce gave away a Ford car, valued at five hundred dollars, to the person who drew the lucky number, and though my work was in the field as land inspector, I'll admit that I lost most of about twelve days, hoping for my car.

One little girl friend of ours, whose parents were in great need, insisted on going to the drawing, over her mother's protest, for she was not dressed as her mother would have liked, but she said, "Mama, I am going to draw that car," and she did. It paid many debts.

Chicago World's Fair, in 1893

Pa came home from the store early that August day in 1893, with the surprising news that I could go to "The Fair." For one or two years we had talked about going to the World's Fair at Chicago, but the hard times made it appear impossible as the time came to go. Chicago was a long way from Hillsboro, Texas. If you think times were never really hard prior to the Depression years of the 1930s, you did not live in a cotton country when the crops had been cut short for years, and the price was down to four cents a pound.

That period has been referred to as the Gay Nineties, yet to me it seemed then, and more so now, as the "Sane Nineties." Though people griped about hard times and blamed Wall Street and the dry weather, they maintained a wholesome attitude toward life, serious enough to concentrate on the essentials, and the church had a strong hold on the best elements of the population.

Conditions were not right for the entire family to make the trip that early in the year because the fall collections had not been made. The farm trade being the big trade for a hardware and implement merchant meant that the bulk of the business was done on "fall time," when collections were made if the farmer made a crop. All notes matured on October 1, by which time the cotton wagons should be rolling to the gin.

When Pa learned that a number of our friends planned to go the next day, he decided that it would be my best chance to see the Fair, as I should be back in school by early September, and he rustled enough money to make it possible. Being fifteen years old and as large as my father, I felt that I could go alone, but he felt it would be wise to have me go with older people. John Turner, who was one of the clerks in the store, was well fitted for my sidekick, as he was a quiet, sensible young man, mature in his ways, and naturally, had an interest in my welfare.

With fifty-five dollars cash, I was ready to catch the daylight train, as our tickets cost twenty-nine dollars, which left me twenty-six dollars for hotels, meals and incidentals for the ten-day trip.

Though four of our party went "Pullman," all the rest went "Chair Car," and took lunches. The M.K.&T. Railroad put on a through train from Galveston, Texas, to Chicago. Never before, and only recently, have any of the railroads run through trains from Texas to Chicago without changes at St. Louis or Kansas City.

John and I found a room at the Deering Hotel, near the fairgrounds. This hotel, a temporary one of about four or five stories, had been built by a harvester company which my father represented. As the price of the room was a dollar a day, we each got off for fifty cents. Naturally, there was no private bath nor elevators. I believe each floor had a bath, however, and the weather was not too warm, even in late August.

Show's Bakery, nearby, prepared a most palatable lunch of buns and baked ham, a hunk of cake and an apple, for thirty cents. At times it cost thirty-five cents, but with two of us to share the cost, we did not pinch on that. Besides, it would have cost us seventy-five cents each to get a meal in the grounds. We tried to finish our program each day early enough to eat supper outside the grounds where restaurants charged a quarter.

John and I usually worked together, but when separated, we would arrange a meeting place for lunch, which I carried in a little grip suspended by a shoulder strap, somewhat like a bag the WAACs later used.

At last my dreams were being realized as we entered the gates and found long lines of people forming on each side of the entrance watching for an impressive parade and the arrival of some dignitaries, perhaps the governor, or the mayor.

While watching the procession, we chatted with a charming lady from Kentucky, whom John, in his droll way, referred to ever afterwords as our "Kentucky Widow." I asked how he knew she was a widow. "During the Fair, son, we have a right to assume that she is either a miss or a widow, and she seems a bit mature for a Miss."

If you have your history on straight, you will know that the Columbian Exposition was a year late in celebrating the four hundredth anniversary of the discovery of America. In browsing through some history of the windy city, I learned that the delay was caused by the financial "Panic" as we called such things before the 1930 Depression. The Fair started a renaissance, so the man said, in Chicago, though we got our first real relief at home several years later.

The schoolteachers who had sought to impress the date of the discovery of America by quoting the rhyme, "In 1492, Columbus sailed the deep, deep blue," heard their pupils chanting, "In 1493, Columbus sailed the deep, deep sea."

This magic city was truly a "white city," as it was called. White buildings, white shell streets, the shimmering lake, and a bright sky overhead made it the next thing to Heaven for me. Most of us had to wear smoked glasses to be comfortable.

The classic architecture prevailing gave a much more pleasing impression than the garish, meaningless slabs of yellow and blue that slammed us in the face at the Chicago Fair forty years later. Maybe I am old-fashioned, yet I wished that those graceful buildings could have been of a permanent nature, as I felt that I would never grow tired of revisiting this fairyland.

Though all the buildings had charm, the exhibits within the California State Building impressed me more than all the rest, with the profusion of fruits and flowers. Outside, a sky-touching flagpole guarded the front of the building.

The Transportation Building was, of course, interesting with its display of every sort of cart, buggy, phaetons, surreys, cabs, coaches and railway trains. It was too early for the automobiles.

The Arts Building was worked in a short while. But at this late date, fifty-eight years later, I remember not the paintings of the masters, but the nude statue of an athlete which I think was posed for by the then-celebrated strong man, Sandow. There was nothing lacking but clothes.

Just at sunrise one morning we rode the giant Ferris wheel, the granddaddy of all ferris wheels, said to have been 275 feet from the ground at the top. Riding in large glass cars, we were able to get a fine view of the grounds, the lake and much of the south part of the city.

The next day we allotted to the sights in Chicago, outside of the grounds.

First came Libby Prison, an old Confederate prison which had been moved, brick for brick, from its home down South to Chicago. No more interesting day was spent than this one. The prison was filled with historic relics, mostly of the Civil War period. Yet, on the floor appeared a great number of brass plates marking the location of prisoners' bunks, as pointed out by the soldiers who had spent months in durance vile.

When noon came, we found a peddler offering big, fine bananas for ten cents a dozen. One dozen satisfied us for lunch.

From the top of Masonic Temple, a twenty-two-story building, "the highest building west of New York," we were able to get a smoky view of the principal business section of the city.

Mr. Bill Knight, another hometown friend, joined me

in another workout of the city. After riding the cable cars serving our part of the city, we rode some horse-drawn streetcars. Uncle Bill was of enquiring mind, so we stood on the platform and learned from the driver that on some streets the law required the use of horses or mules, perhaps because of narrow streets, though I am not sure such was the reason.

The stockyards inspection was an eye-opener to me. I then learned what happened to our longhorns which were shipped to the packing houses.

The real high point was the Buffalo Bill's Wild West Show. Here we saw the Battle of Little Big Horn, the stage-coach robbery, and the wonderful shooting by Bill Cody and Miss Annie Oakley, the "greatest woman shot in the world." She really did some shooting. One other famous shot appeared, whose name I have forgotten, though it may have been Dr. Carver, who a few years before had been known as the champion of the world. Dr. Carver, when I saw him in a circus in my hometown, had long, dark curls, reaching to his shoulders, so I think this man must have been a later development.

Two days was all I could spare outside the grounds. I had to see more of the Fair before my supply of money ran out.

One afternoon was spent watching aquatic sports. First came the battle between two flat-bottomed scows, each six-man crew being armed with a fire hose and seeking to sink the other ship. It seemed a near even fight for quite awhile until some giant in one boat standing in one corner caused it to take water and sink.

As the losing team floundered in the water, the hose still spouting a stream in every direction, the judges rowed out in a small boat to award the prize. The high silk hats and long black coats lost much luster when the stream of water soaked their boat.

The cavalry duel came next. Each horseman was mounted on a barrel having a horse's head and tail. A breastplate hung from a cord around his neck, and he carried a shield, also a broom, which served as a weapon and as an oar. The battle was spirited, and the big fellow who had sunk his own boat found it impossible to mount after he had been unhorsed. Some enemy would jab him about the time he had the barrel standing on end, while he tried to mount.

That night, the brilliant display of fireworks surpassed anything I had ever seen. While the rockets soared, searchlights from the four corners of the Government Building played over the crowd. That was the only time that trouble threatened me. From the end of that pier, the water looked dark and deep as a belligerent man and I jockeyed for a favorable position.

Had I seen nothing else, the vision of the West Point Corps at retreat would have justified the long trip for me. On Government Plaza, between the Government Building and the lake, was a white-tented city, the temporary home of the corps toward which my dreams had pointed. One of our Hillsboro boys, Tom Stroud, was a cadet, and was I a proud visitor to his tent.

Sunset always found me watching retreat, as the C.O. boomed his commands and each white-gloved hand moved in unison through the manual of arms. That picture is still vivid in my memory — long lines of soldierly figures in high hats, dark coats, and white trousers standing there while Old Glory came down, "Just as the Sun Went Down."

My soldierly dreams were never realized, but the love of military history, born many years before that, has never waned. It was born when the late Maj. Gen. Beaumont B. Buck, whose parents lived in our town, became a cadet and acquired a national reputation by shooting one of the boys who sought to haze him just before he entered the academy. Through all those years, from the time privates earned fourteen dollars a month to this day, I have watched the record of men of arms.

The day John and I spent in the city, he developed a thirst, and we entered a basement beer parlor, where John ordered a beer. Being reared in a Methodist home, and having had certain definite rules of conduct impressed upon me, I declined to order. As the lady in black tights appeared on the stage, I was interested in staying, but the waiter advised me with some firmness that "We do not entertain visitors."

I urged John to enjoy his beer, and I would wait for him on the street, but he refused and passed up this opportunity for relief. Though our friendship has lasted through long lives, I have never thought to ask him just what his opinion of me was that evening.

One of our boys, Guy Brooks, had a flair for night life and joined a companion whom he had met on the train coming to Chicago, and found some games of chance in progress. Guy saw that his companion was losing his shirt, so when he was invited to join in the game, he told his hosts that his father had all his money. After being cleaned of his cash, Rastur asked Guy to let him have five dollars to get home on, as he had a round-trip ticket, but had to leave that night, promising to meet Guy's homecoming train at Fort Worth and make restitution. When I learned of this, I asked Guy what Rastur's other name was. He did not know. He did not know that he had any name except the name Rastur, which Guy had given him. Believe it or not, a few nights later, as our train pulled into Fort Worth, there was Rastur with his five-dollar bill.

The weather those last two weeks in August 1893 was perfect for me except about two days, when a sharp, cold wind blew in from the lake and chilled me in my salt and pepper summer suit, making my big sailor straw look out of place. Now, that hat was really something to see. I felt that I was setting the style for all the country. It was heavy, hard-pressed straw, about one-fourth of an inch thick, with a wing spread of six inches beyond the fuselage. To avoid decapitating some passerby, I had it held by a black cable which was anchored to my lapel.

The description of the "Midway Piaisance" cannot be given, as I merely viewed the shows thereon from the center of the street leading through its exotic area. But doubtless you have seen many such which have since been labeled carnivals at the street fairs.

Many times have I visited Chicago since then, but no

other visit brought the pleasures growing out of a visit to the Columbian Exposition in 1893. Then boys were not surfeited with all the sights and sounds which fill the eyes and ears of the sophisticated youth of today; hence, there was much that was to me awe-inspiring, such as the booming pipe organ and the fireworks, and the silent gondoliers gliding through lagoons that surrounded the enchanted island, that might appear commonplace to present-day boys.

The Fair doubtless meant more to me than to other members of my family, who did not go until the weather was so cold that my brothers said they spent much of their time down in the boiler rooms trying to keep warm. After nearly eighty years, I can still see the crescent lake, the fireworks, the graceful buildings, the West Point boys and the enchanted island among the lagoons.

The *Review of Reviews* of September 1893 contains some interesting comments on the Fair and general financial conditions, as appears below:

> The two best months of year for the World's Fair yet remain. Undoubtedly the severe business depression has made the summer attendance much smaller than it otherwise would have been.
>
> The Fair will fall far short of financial success that was originally expected of it.
>
> The railroads will be inclined to a liberal policy in the weeks that remain, and Chicago will be disposed to make board and lodging as reasonable as possible for visitors.
>
> The stoppage of business has given many a man a welcome vacation who might, if he had the courage to spend a part of his little savings to use this period of enforced idleness in a trip to Chicago. . . .
>
> General advice cannot be given to fit each individual, but many a man will testify that the best thing that ever came to him was a temporary freedom and leisure entailed by hard times and stoppage of work and machinery.

Many a man is weighed down with anxiety about the disposition of accumulated funds. He is afraid of the Savings Banks, and a deposit in the cupboard drawer or between the mattresses brings up ugly fears of burglary and fire. Why not put some of this troublesome money into a permanently paying and solid investment, as a trip to the World's Fair? It will pay well.

The Ferris Wheel

Since the Ferris wheel was such a striking accomplishment of engineering skill and daring, I deemed it advisable to make a little research on the subject: first, to check with my recollection of the figures as to the height, which I found to be correct, and then to learn how it had come about. A most interesting account appears in the *Review of Reviews* of that year, from which I will quote a few paragraphs. The report was by Carl Snyder.

George Washington Fale Ferris, the inventor of the great Ferris Wheel, was a young engineer who sketched the design over a cup of coffee, and it is said the wheel was built exactly as planned in this sketch.

After all its spectacular qualities are dismissed, the wheel is a triumph of modern engineering. It brings into play a new mechanical principle and exhibits the almost limitless possibilities of steel construction.

It was born of an obvious want. When the big fair was planned there came up from the whole nation one well-nigh universal demand — that was for some novel achievement which would discount the Eiffel Tower. Something striking and original. It was a Macedonian call.

The young engineer's proposal was for a perfect pinion wheel 250 feet in diameter. It was to be a tension wheel; that is to say, a wheel with tension and not solid spokes. His brother engineers said it could not be done.

On December 28 every scrap of iron was pig. On June 21, less than six months later, 2200 tons of this pig, converted into a revolving mechanism as perfect a pinion wheel as an Elgin watch, began to turn on its 70 ton axis, and has been turning ever since, without creak or crack.

The towers, eight in number, are thirty feet square and thirty feet high, of solid cement. Buried in the concrete are massive steel bars, and to them are bolted the steel towers. 268 feet in the air reaches the wheel above the earth. It is equipped with thirty-six cars, with a total capacity of one thousand people.

To test the effective resistance to wind, Mr. and Mrs. Ferris, and reporter took a ride during the storm described as follows:

The test was the terrific hurricane which swept Chicago in July. It was a straight north and south gale, and it struck the wheel fairly across its face.

Slowly the giant wheel lifted them into the midst of the roaring tempest. As the mad storm swept around the cars, the blast was deafening. It screamed through the spider-like girders and shook the windows with savage fury. It was a place to try men's nerves. The engineer and his wife had faith in his wheel. The reporter, at that moment, believed neither in God nor man.

But the beautiful wheel hardly shivered. It turned as evenly and as smoothly as if fanned by a summer breeze. The headlong gale, plunging against us at 110 miles an hour could not cause a perceptible deflection in its course.

I Saw the Sun Set on a Century

I watched the sun go down on a turbulent century: four major wars involving all the states, in addition to the

Texas revolution against Mexico, and almost continuing Indian wars, little and big, through many periods of the century's history.

Physical destruction by fires, storms and earthquakes wrecking cities, and fierce political battles — some leading up to the fratricidal war between the states, devastating droughts and sandstorms, financial panics.

The Spanish-America War was about over, and the horizon seemed to offer an early peaceful expansion of growth and industry. We welcomed the coming of the sunrise of another century. People seemed very happy and hopeful for the future.

The year 1899, however, proved a most distressing one for me and one of my brothers, while we were operating a stock and grain farm in Hardeman County on the fringe of the Texas Panhandle. Every hard lick the weatherman could devise hit us — unprecedented blizzards in the early months, followed by drying winds which blew the wheat out of the ground and started storms, and, at harvest time, torrential rains ruined the wheat. Yet we survived and began to start anew.

Now, we will shift the scene to a sunrise, and a change of tempo, to storytelling relating to the first few years of the twentieth century. Selah.

AFTER THE SUNRISE

III

After the Sunrise

Mrs. Henrietta King

It was my good fortune to receive an invitation to visit the famed King Ranch, in Kleburg County, Texas, in the spring of 1923, and to meet the venerable lady, Mrs. Henrietta King, her daughter Mrs. Alice Kleburg and her husband, and the Kleburg children.

The invitation came through Mrs. King's brother, Mr. Edwin Chamberlain of San Antonio, to a group of us who were connected with the First National Bank of Chicago, two vice-presidents, and one or two employees. Mr. Chamberlain and I were soon thereafter to share the same office suite. Also with our group was Mr. Chamberlain's son Edmund, who was to be associated with me as Federal Land Appraiser. He was a helpful member of our party.

We reached the ranch one March morning while the ranch people were rounding up and branding cattle. Mrs. Alice Kleburg acted as hostess because her mother was then ninety years old, but we had the pleasure of Mrs. King's company at a delicious dinner at the long table in the big house, where efficient Mexican help gave us the most courteous service.

Mr. Robert Kleburg joined us at the noon dinner table, but he was in poor health and left the entertaining largely to others.

Two or more of the Misses Kleburg joined us. One of the young ladies had been helping the cowboys in the round-up, so came clad in a rough khaki riding outfit and a man's slouch hat. Each member of the family was raised in the saddle.

Robert and Richard Kleburg, with the aid of a cousin, Caesar Kleburg, with the permission of Mrs. King and Mr. and Mrs. Kleburg, operated the ranch. Robert gave all of his time to the work, and Richard was quite an active lawyer, politician, and public relations man. He later was a member of Congress who was once served by a noted man in the political field, Lyndon Johnson, as secretary.

There was a common bond between Richard (Dick) Kleburg and me, because we had attended The University of Texas at the same time, though we did not get well acquainted until later.

We were driven around parts of this kingdom, which has really served Texas as a most valuable experimental farm and ranch. The one-time valuable Rhodes grass, which served South Texas ranchmen for many years, was introduced and grown on this ranch. And, the only American breed of cattle, the Santa Gertrudis, followed the years of painstaking crossbreeding until a distinct breed was produced, which is now worldwide in its popularity.

Famous race horses have since been developed there too. Since that visit in 1923, I have visited the ranch more than once, and enjoyed the hospitality of this generous family in this great house. I regard this ranch as part of the Texas heritage which has served Texas long and usefully.

For forty-three years I had waited for some master hand to write the story of the King Ranch, and the strong-willed pioneers who gave it to us as a heritage. Now, I have been rewarded by Tom Lea of our own Hill Country, who has told the story as I believe no other person could tell it, and if this little essay can stimulate any reader to read this two-volume story of how that part of the West was won, I will feel rewarded.

Two years, almost to the day, after my first visit to the King Ranch, Mrs. Henrietta King died, on March 31, 1925.

Tom Lea's description of the closing of the life of this great lady should create a thirst for the full story of the ranch and its people, so I take the liberty of copying it with the hopes that it may inspire someone and add to his knowledge of Texas history as it was made.

> Death came to her, at the age of ninety-two at about ten o'clock on a spring night, at the Santa Gertrudis, March 31, 1925.
>
> Her body lay in state in a bronze casket, in the lower-big front room of her great house, while her family, her friends, her employees came to the rise on the prairie where she had lived for seventy brave and useful years. Messages to her family sped along the wires leading to Kingsville. Relatives and friends arrived on iron rails from the four quarters, from far cities. News of the death travelled over country roads, carried by lips of sunburned drivers, behind the wheels of dusty, brush-scratched automobiles, men with harness reins in their hard hands, men spurred sweated horses through tall grass and thickets of thorn to rough settlements and lonely camps.
>
> From the furtherest corners of far South Texas pastures, there began a great convergence on Santa Gertrudis. Men came with their wide-brimmed hats in their hands. They brought their wives, who dabbed damp handkerchiefs at weather-rough faces. They brought their solemn-faced children. They parked their wagons and their cars to camp on the grass and under the trees.
>
> All the Kinenos came. Some of them rode their horses two days and a night to arrive on time.

The foremen of the cow camps gathered as a body at the headquarters, and went to present themselves to Alice Kleburg, to express their sorrow formally and in the ancient style to La Mandama's daughter; to pledge again their faithfulness to her family.

A great throng crowded to the simple funeral at the big house on April 4th, at three thirty in the sunny afternoon. When the service, conducted by the Rev. S. E. Chandler was concluded a cortege more than a mile long moved behind the black hearse down the gentle slope from the Santa Gertrudis on the road to town, to the cemetery of Kingsville, which Henrietta King had planted, and named Chamberlain Park in honor of her father.

An honor guard unlike any other on the face of the earth led the slow procession. The ranch cowboys, nearly two hundred of them, wearing their ranch clothes, riding their range horses, accompanied La Patrona, who had always been their partisan, upon the final journey.

At her crowded graveside, during the hymns, eulogies and last prayers, grey-haired bankers from Manhattan rubbed shoulders with leather-faced brush choppers from the lonely callos of El Sauz.

When the casket was lowered into the earth there was a stir in the edge of the crowd where the bareheaded horsemen stood. They mounted to their saddles. They came reining forward in single file, unbidden and uncommanded save by their hearts, to canter, with a centaur dash once around the open grave, their hats down at side salute to Henrietta King. Then the vaqueros rode away in silence, toward the herds they had watched for her and would go on watching.

Eighty-Nine Miles from Dawn to Dusk

Did you ever spend a midsummer week driving through

the mountains of northern Mexico in a heavy three-seated hack, over ungraded trails? Did you ever spend a night lying on a tarp spread on the gravelly slope of an arroyo, and, because you were too cold to sleep, get up at 4 A.M. to sit beside Juan, the vaquero, as he sat crosslegged on the dry ground, smoking his homemade cigarette and silently watching the coffee in the pot coming to a boil on a mesquite wood fire?

After daylight breakfast, did you thrill to the crisp morning ride in the rarefied air until you got chilled enough to get out and trot along beside the hack, to keep up with the six little Spanish mules?

If so, you will have some understanding of the conditions in the land where José Torres and Tomás Zafiro lived and learned to run all day in order to get the deer they were needing for food.

It will help you to know how Lola Cuzarare, the fourteen-year-old girl, was able to cover a distance of twenty-eight miles (from San Marcos to Austin) in four hours and fifty-five minutes, in the astonishing race from San Antonio to the Memorial Stadium, in Austin, between dawn and dusk.

It was a Friday, March 24, 1927 at 3:19 A.M. when José Torres and Tomás Zafiro started on their race to the Memorial Stadium, in Austin, Texas, eighty-nine miles away.

Excerpts from the report of the Austin correspondent of the *San Antonio Express* of March 25, 1927 tell more of the details of this record-breaking race.

José Torres and Tomás Zafiro, the men, started from San Antonio, at 3:19 o'clock in the morning, and crossed the finish line in the stadium, at 6:12 o'clock, Friday night, making their time for eighty-nine and four-tenths miles, fourteen hours and fifty-three minutes.

Lola Cuzarare finished the twenty-eight miles in four hours and fifty-five minutes. Zafiro delivered to Fielding H. Yost, Michigan football coach and relay game official, a letter for Governor Dan Moody, from Mayor J. W. Tobin, of San Antonio, commenting on the age-old custom of using runners for messengers in war and peace, complimenting the Indians, and wishing the Governor success.

The men battled their way to the finish line through a barrage of carbon monoxide gas from hundreds of automobiles that congested the highways, a stiff gale which tired and retarded them, and heat to which they were not accustomed in their native mountains of Mexico. They were unaccustomed to the hard surfaced highway and the rough gravel roads over which their course led them, and were forced to wear sandals, but they never varied the easy rhythm of their stride except when they stopped for an olive oil rub or for food. In their first hour they covered about six miles, and this pace was increased until they were running faster than seven miles an hour at times. Within twenty miles of the finish, however, they were surrounded by hundreds of automobiles, which laid down dense layers of carbon monoxide gas and got in their way. This slowed them down so seriously that they were unable to make more than four miles an hour toward the end. . . . They jogged along steadily, reeling off mile after mile, as the sun shone hotter and hotter, and the highway gleamed with the heat. Their reddish brown bodies glistened in the sun, as they pattered along through curious throngs, especially in the towns. . . . Bright shirts and sweaters which they wore at the start were discarded as the day progressed, and they soon donned broad sombreros. Each carried a piece of cane as they ran; they ate some of their native food, and they called for water, which was given them. It was given them out of a dipper without stopping, or it was dashed on their bodies.

The girl who finished her course, which measured a little over twenty-eight miles, showed little signs of fatigue, and ran once around the stadium track while the thousands at the games cheered her. She walked off the field steadily and smilingly.

Some of the men and some of the women who started with the winners were compelled to drop out before reaching their goal.

Before the reader challenges the report of the distance between the start and the finish, keep in mind this happened forty years ago, when the course was over the legendary "Post Road" from San Antonio to Austin. The distance, however, was eighty-two miles, which I measured many times by car odometer. This was before the highway engineers had cut down the hills, and filled up the valleys, and made straight the charming black-top road that wound its way through the timbered hills, and down into the valleys, and across the low concrete dips at the little mountain streams.

When man sees what man has wrought with his bulldozers and his road graders and pushing the forest back, robbing the scenery of the fields of bluebonnets that skirted the edges of the narrow roadways, he loses sight of much that God has wrought.

He has reduced time and space with his wide highways, and his seventy-mile-an-hour speed, but he has deprived men and women of today of much that was rich and charming in the lives of those of forty years ago, when charming San Antonio offered a relaxing atmosphere and a feel for history.

Reading the names involved in this story stirs the memories of three most colorful men: The charming politician and city builder, Mayor Bill Tobin, the brilliant governor, Dan Moody, and "Hurry Up Yost," the Michigan coach, who was known to all sports lovers.

This happened, mind you, in the booming twenties, when few people could see the rainbow's end that touched the earth that October day in 1929, and left the world in darkness.

As residents of San Antonio, we watched the building of the Mayor's Pride, the wonderful auditorium, with unexcelled acoustics; the Masonic Temple of magnificent proportions; the Olmos Dam, and the new hotels and office buildings. The first all-air-conditioned office building in Texas, the Milam Bulding, was a standout.

Now, as the new year 1968 begins, I can read about the fleet-footed trackmen, with a record of 9.1 on one hundred yards, and several men over the globe who can cover the mile in less than four minutes, and a giant A&M boy who can toss the shot over seventy feet, but I know of no one who can match the endurance test of those simple Mexican Indians in their long-distance race.

Feud on Forty Acres

Sixty-one years have wiped out the picture for those not old enough to remember the Forty Acres, as the home of The University of Texas was then known. Yet, the picture is clear in my memory, as a law student, in the spring of 1906.

The old administration building that housed the law department in its basement, and *academes* above, has long since been destroyed, the beautiful rolling campus with its green turf, sprinkled with bluebonnets, Indian paintbrush, and wine-cups, has been buried under concrete and steel and brick buildings.

Judge B. D. Tarlton, the tall, corpulent, patrician professor of law, paused for a moment in his lecture on real estate, and smiled his winning smile, as one of our leading "Laws" came late into the lecture room. On the high brow of our fellow Law was a sign, "C. E. '08," the brand of the uncouth Engineers, who had captured Haynie the night before and waltzed him over the hills, much to his humiliation.

After the class had been dismissed, the fearful wrath of

the Laws resulted in appointing a committee for a search and seizure of the low-born Engineers, who laid unholy hands on a Law. I was too old to participate in this undertaking, being then at the age of twenty-eight, but I followed the developments with interest.

During the guerrilla war it was not very safe for either an Engineer or junior Law to appear alone on the campus at night, for fear the hue and cry might start a rabbit race, as one side or the other group might start the chase by crying "Junior Law, Junior Law," or "Engineer, Engineer."

In due course, the leader was captured and summary punishment was dealt him, and as evidence, a flashlight picture was brought to Judge Tarlton's class one morning, showng a tall Engineer, dressed in his underclothes, with a coating of molasses and feathers.

Our dean of the law school, Judge Miller, a quiet, dignified gentleman, appeared before the Laws, and told them this matter had gone far enough. He did not want to act as policeman, but he let it be known that no more such monkeyshines would be permitted.

In later years, I got a story from Dick Kleburg, who claimed to be one of the captors of the leaders, C. E. Scoggins. He said they caught him as he was getting in a cab to attend a fraternity dance.

Many, many years later, I wrote to a C. E. Scoggins, after reading his most interesting stories about the Incas, and such other vanished tropical temple builders, and asked him if he was the man who laid unholy hands on a junior Law. If so, I said, "All is forgiven," and invited him back to Texas. I cherish the fine responsive letter he wrote me. He confessed, but thought he gave as much as he received, and thanked me for inviting him back home, as the following letter indicates:

Dear Mr. Thompson:

Thanks for yours of November 12, duly forwarded to me by the Saturday Evening Post (but not very promptly acknowledged by me because I'm pretty busy framing a new story) about "MAN LOST." It always pleases me to hear from anybody who enjoys my stories, and especially from those who share old memories with me.

I was indeed the Scoggins who participated in the laying on of hands — but not unholy hands! the righteous, virtuous, corrective hands of engineers — upon the person of a man misguided enough to study law. For "hands", of course, read "T-square"; and for "person of a man" read "person of any man we could catch unguarded." But I know which one you mean. His name was Haynes or Haynie; there was one of each, but the one you have in mind was like yourself an older man; I can remember yet how disconcerted I was to walk into his room — I'd never seen him — and find him of an age that entitled him to be called "sir." He was an M.A. returning for a law course; but a junior law just the same, so I heaved him over a balcony into the hands of my confederates lurking in the rose bushes. . . . He was afterward taken into my fraternity, Phi Gamma Delta. . . . It's quite true that I fell victim to foul persecution at the hands of lawless laws; it can't be called retribution — because I dealt out in my time more grief than I received. Ah, me, them was the days!

I have somewhere in my possession yet a piece of the original Peregrinus — only we called it Pereginoose; remember? — a leather banner with brass studs outlining the fabled figure, half starved cat, half wolf; it was torn from the walls of the law library by the Fillilooloo Band. I also have a piece of the original Alexander Frederick Claire, which was stolen from the Engineering building by laws and recovered by burglary and hidden over half the State of Texas before he was cut up and distributed to end the feud; the man who sent me my piece was none other than T. U. Taylor, then still Dean of the Engineering School. He remembered how often — and how unjustly! — he'd had me on the carpet in my student days, and handsomely made amends by sending me a small bronze replica of Alec. Maybe you remember: Alec in person was a huge wooden statue of Gambrinus, stolen from Jacoby's beer garden, adopted as the patron saint of the Engineers and named from the immortal ditty of Sunny Jim Sims — the engineer who, looking over his shoulder at a co-ed in the Academic Building, fell downstairs and broke both his legs.

Oh, well, I guess the times don't change much! The University of Colorado is in this town, and undergraduates still sing,

> Here's to our college,
> To hell with the knowledge
> We get at the U of C!

Misguided, perhaps, but I don't frown. My personal motto is "Forsanet haec olim meminisse iuvabit" — you know: maybe some day these things too will be fun to remember.

Glad to have heard from you. If I come your way, I'll try to find your "house by the side of the road."

Sincerely yours,
C. E. Scoggins

Mogul Robinson

Mogul Robinson was an athlete to be remembered by all who love the traditions of The University of Texas. No adequate story is possible in the limited space allotted to this essay, yet it may serve to stimulate enquiry for a fuller story of this speed merchant and fine gentleman whose life story became more romantic after he left college than at the height of his football career. I was a junor Law in the spring of 1906 when he was at the zenith of his athletic career. But I will let Judge Ireland Graves tell the story better than I can. He graduated in law in 1906. His letter to the chairman of the Selection Committee, Longhorn Hall of Honor follows:

Robbie was built for football, and was a halfback without superior. . . . There were no defensive nor offensive teams. He played both places equally well. In spite of his stocky build, being 5'8", weight 158 lbs., he was also a track star, and in the 1905 Southwestern track meet, he won three medals: gold, silver and bronze.

Robin's day of glory was the day of Texas' most ignominious defeat . . . on November 4th, against the University of Chicago, on Marshall Field. The Chicago team, coached by Amos Alonzo Stagg, and with the immortal Eckersall as quarterback, won the game by 68 to 0. On Sunday, November 6, the *Chicago Tribune* was adorned with Don Robinson's picture, with this sketch.

ROBINSON STARS FOR TEXAS

Robinson starred for Texas on offense, and did the greater part of the punting, besides. A peculiar formation was used, in kicking; Robinson punting from the regular half-back position without stepping back. His punts were high and short, enabling his ends to get under them easily.

The Texans started off with a rush, and by successive bucks, waded through the Chicago line, to their fifty yard line. He, Robinson, broke loose and circling left end, ran forty yards before being downed by Eckersall, on Chicago's twenty yard line. Then came a fumble by Texas, followed by a recovery, and a touchdown by Eckersall. Robinson advanced the ball a total of 93 yards for Texas during the game.

Aside from the defeat by Chicago, and another Texas loss 4 to 0 to the Haskell Indians, Texas had an undefeated season for the remaining five teams. At the end of the 1905-06 year, he received his law degree, and was lost to college athletics forever. I doubt if there was ever a more loved man on the campus. . . . He had three nicknames, Robbie, Rosy and Mogul, from his way of plowing through an opposing team, reminding us of the Mogul engines of the day. Those who knew him will not forget him. He was not only a Longhorn of genius, but a fine sportsman and a great gentleman.

In July 1923, the *Alcalde*, published by the Alumni Association of The University of Texas, carried an interesting story written by a schoolmate of the well-known athlete, Mogul Robinson. Parts of this letter furnish us with a picture of how Robinson appeared to his close college associates. This is quoted from a letter written by R. R. Smith, '08.

He said his name was Don Robinson. George C. Butte, Registrar, fearing enough to write his own

name like this, George C. F. Butte, solemnly registered him as Don Robinson. As he was born in
Missouri . . . he came whirling in ahead of everybody else on the field at the first fall athletic try-
out, running like a frightened fawn, and puffing
like a locomotive. Somebody yelled for "The
Mogul," and Mogul he was forever afterward, except to the Registrar.

Mogul was shaped like a Greek statue, cast in
wax that had stood in the sun and settled down
evenly to wide proportions. His head was wide
at the top. His nose distinctly Greek, but a bit
heavy. His cheeks regular, but of an Irish rud-
diness. His hair, a Scottish sandy, and rather thin.
His eyes as blue as a vestal virgin's, and equally as
guileless. His lips, full, but still faintly marked
with a cupid's bow. His feet were small but fleet.
His dress slightly careless, indifferent to everything
but neatness. His habits were abstemious. He had
no vice at all, and only one weakness. He could not
handle himself around the ladies.

As a football player, Mogul was a nonpareil of his generation. He had the fearlessness of a wolverine, the craftiness
of a fox, and the speed of a beagle. He was an individual
hero of every attendant at the university, and he ran from
praise as an egotist runs from ridicule.

Hal Logan, also from Missouri, was something of a
gallant. One night he persuaded Robinson to go out with
him for a call on two comely co-eds. Their names are not
material.

The ladies were cordially grateful to Hal for bringing
this hero into their parlor. Hal tried to handle the conversation, when Mogul went into the silence of confused
modesty. But the ladies pumped Mogul, ignoring Hal. He
answered yes or no as the question would permit, and
twisted around on his chair sizing up the furniture and the
decorations. Never a line of live conversation could he utter.

Finally, one of the ladies, seeking to excuse his evident

lack of ease and chatter, inquired with bright inspiration, "You don't go out socially very often, do you, Mr. Robinson?"

"No, by gum!" came the explosive answer to the surprise and confusion of everybody present. "Hal got me into this."

It was a knockout. Hal swore he would never take Mogul out again, and Mogul swore he never should.

In the December *Alcalde*, of 1924, is a long letter from Don Robinson, written from his plantation home in Zamboanga, Philippines, addressed to the editor.

Dear Friend:

Your letter of 30th reached me in due time, and in due time, as reckoned in this land of mañana, I answer you. Perhaps you will say that stretching mañana for five months is a little too far. Then hear me, my friend. Did you ever try to plant ten thousand coconuts in one season, with only moroes to help you? If you ever had, you would excuse me, even though mañana stretched out for five months, was extended to Pasado mañana.

Also my tardiness in making remittance to the *Alcalde*, would, I suppose, indicate that I do not appreciate it. But, I want you to know that I do appreciate it very much; more than you could know unless you were here yourself.

My wife and boy went to the States last spring, and it will be a year, perhaps more, before I see them again. With them away, I do not come in touch with, or speak the language of civilization, as I would if they were here. So, in this land of primitive minds the coming of the *Alcalde* is a reminder that at one time, the University of Texas made efforts to civilize me. Occasionally, under the certain promptings and memories, I find traces of that old civilization yet. About three years ago, in answer to a request you vicariously made, I wrote you a long letter, telling of some of the things of life here in the Philippines. That letter, we must assume, was the result of an urge of the old culture that the University sought to impress upon me. You remember the letter, I believe, for you saw fit to publish it in the *Alcalde*.

Then you wrote me on two other occasions, asking that I make other contributions. I never answered your letters. I offer no apology, but let me explain. You were too flattering. You almost made me believe that I could write, and that there was someone interested in what I had to say. For many days I built air castles about your honeyed words. They almost made me forget the jungle that waited to be cleared and planted.

I dream of what might have been had I followed the path in which the University tried to set my feet, instead of reverting to an age long since dead and gone. Beware how you use your flattery. Everyone has his place in life. False notions cause misfits. I am in my element here; in the cave of my pre-historic ancestor of whom I spoke to you before. But for him I might have yielded to your temptings, for he has drawn very near to me, and jealously shields me from all influences that would tend to weaken the ties and traditions of the old cave life.

The above is a small part of a most interesting letter.

Pioneer Bird Men

The British and Canadian flyers, stationed at the Fort Worth flying field, were the pioneers in the air fifty years ago; that is, they made us all conscious of what was yet to come.

The first overseas cap, such as were later adopted by all our American servicemen, were first worn by these aviators.

Later, our own boys were training there in those biplanes. The first flying hero in our town of Hillsboro was Jerry Clark, who flew down for a few minutes' visit to the home folks, and we gathered in the pasture adjoining Capt. A. P. McKinnon's home, to greet Jerry as he flew in and parked his ship for a handshaking few minutes. Then he rose from the cow pasture turf, circled around a bit, dived toward the little lake, or pond, and let loose a volley of machine gun blasts into the water; finally he lifted his nose, and was soon in the wild blue yonder.

Some time later, I wanted to share the thrill of flying, and paid ten bucks to a barnstormer for a ten-minute ride over the hometown. I asked him how high we were at one point, and he said about fifteen hundred feet. The rig was a two-seater, with me in the front, in an open cockpit, and no belt or place to hold to except the edge of the cockpit. When he nosed down, the chocolate-covered squares or triangles and rectangles began shooting cotton stalks up, which thrilled me, yet made me mighty ready to get out on the good earth again.

Another exciting occasion, which had a tragic ending, was when a daredevil barnstormer rose from the Courthouse Square, or the nearby street, and circled the area, then flew back down again.

The first day made me uneasy for fear he might not be so lucky the next day, and I decided that on the following day I would get behind one of the big concrete posts. The poor fellow came out of the side street, and at the corner of the square, his right wing tipped just enough to graze a few spectators; then he saw that he was going to fall, and directed his ship straight into some big trees bordering the Courthouse Square. His plane hit the tree limbs, and he shot to earth like a bullet and was promptly taken to the nearest drugstore where doctors waited on him. I never learned just how badly hurt he was, but it was reported that he broke his ankle.

The casualties drifted into the drugstore to get scratches touched up, and some were calm, while some were very much excited. One man, walking toward the drugstore, held his hand to his back, followed by his sympathizing friends; he was groaning and said, "Boys, my back is broken."

Rich Field, at Waco, was another nearby flying bunch

of boys, some with artistic talent. A group of them came to Hillsboro one night and gave a most entertaining show in the basement of the First Methodist Church. All of it was good stuff, but the number that impressed me most, and which has been remembered, is the rendition of "Sextette from Lucia," all on the baseball field, and in baseball language. Two boys playing opposite each other gave us a real operatic performance, from positions as pitcher, catcher, or first baseman. They had real talent.

In another chapter, I hope to continue describing the ways of the gallant men of the air, back when aviation was young.

In a flashback I recall seeing the first flight from coast to coast, by a man named Rogers, who passed over in the autumn of 1911. We watched from the roof of the Citizens National Bank, as the flyer followed the railroad track from Dallas to Hillsboro, then from Hillsboro to Waco.

I wonder how many people remember the lighted routes to guide the night flyers. High towers, with revolving lights, marked the route of passage of later flyers. While I was driving from San Antonio to Austin one cloudy night I thought a big electrical storm was on, as the tower lights kept flashing against the curtain overhead.

The Fly Boys had really become accomplished performers by the time we moved to San Antonio, in the year 1923, and we enjoyed watching them every time we passed Brooks Field or the later established field.

By that time the ships had been much improved in structure and appearance, and were called "Silver Wings," which appeared to me to be very appropriate, as I drove past Brooks Field in the early mornings and saw them soaring over the highway and rising into the early sunlight. It was a beautiful sight, though at times I wished they would not fly quite so close to the top of my car. It was like watching graceful birds, dashing either singly, or in formation, with the sun turning them into first silver, then gold.

On one occasion we drove out to Camp Bullis to watch maneuvers and a sham battle, in which all arms except the cavalry took part. As my wife and my father and I sat on the hillside, watching the advancing soldiers head toward a cluster of mesquite trees, we met Maj. Gen. Beaumont B. Buck, retired, one of the spit-and-polish sort, a gallant, courtly gentleman of the old school.

General Buck was a man of special interest to us old-timers of Hillsboro, for we had watched his career from the time he was appointed to West Point, back in the early 1880s. He had a sensational start, because he shot one of the men who were hazing him, or about to start. Fortunately, the man recovered. Though it did not add to Buck's popularity at the academy, it created quite a sensation over the country, and we of the South, who had not yet forgotten the results of the war, only about twenty years behind us, and the Carpetbag days, were proud that a Texas boy would not submit to overbearing yankees.

The general's autobiography, entitled *Memories of Peace and War*, gives the details of this affair. He saw service in the Spanish-American War, and first world war, and had retired, to live in San Antonio. He was a pleasing speaker. We heard him make a most interesting talk at the Laurel Heights Methodist Church one night.

On another occasion, we drove to the hills to see the making of *Wings*, a most spectacular moving picture, and here the flyers swept over the hills and valleys, and I believe that was the first time I ever saw smoke screens laid by the airmen.

Another interesting motion picture was produced in San Antonio while we lived there. It was *Rough Riders.*

We drove to the old S. P. Depot, where the Rough Riders were taking the train on their start to Cuba. Mary Astor was the leading lady. We watched her walk along beside the waiting train, while townspeople, dressed in the 1898 gear, brought the soldiers baskets of lunch. It was an authentic picture. I was able to judge, as I had been anxious to join Teddy's troop, that spring of 1898, but yielded to appeals to stay in school to get my diploma.

The producers of those two plays stated that nowhere

else in the world, except in Italy, were the skies so well suited to the production of moving pictures.

My first cross-country flight was taken during the 1930s, after I had moved to Dallas. I boarded the plane in San Antonio, with only one other passenger, a young man sitting in the seat just in front of mine. I took a *Saturday Evening Post* with me, thinking I would read, but became too interested in studying the contours of the winding rivers below me and the roads over which little ants seemed to be scurrying. Then, instead of looking up to study the "Buttermilk clouds," I looked down on this white floor below the ship. Now and then, when we ran into a cloud, I felt a drop, like an elevator drop might feel.

The young companion, who seemed so sophisticated, reached back, and asked if he might read my *Post*, which I gladly allowed. But it was not long until I noticed he had laid it down, and opened the window to allow the discharge from a stricken stomach.

On my next trip from San Antonio to Dallas, I rode in a taxi with a man who was about to take his first airborne trip. He was quite anxious to learn if I had ever flown. When I reported that I had been up once, he was quite anxious to know if I got sick. I told him that the ride did not affect me that way, but it did some people, and that I thought mental worry might have contributed to the illness. He replied that he had fortified himself with a good stiff slug before leaving home. I noticed that when we stopped for awhile at Austin, he again fortified himself, and I think that may have relieved the tension, so that he could go to sleep.

In the summer of 1931 or 1932, I took a flight from Dallas to Amarillo. We had a full load of oilmen as far as Wichita Falls, but after that, a young lady and I were the only passengers. She sat near the front of the car, and I was parked near the rear. When we were about halfway between Wichita Falls and Amarillo, I noticed the lady slump down as though she was sick, and I walked to her side and asked if I could help in any way, and I knew of nothing to do but wet a handkerchief with cold water and put it to her throat. I knew of no way to communicate with the pilot, who was not in a position to leave his post if he knew the trouble. I was relieved to note that she rested quietly and was able to leave the ship under her own power.

In a Lighter Vein
Frustrated Gallants

On my way to St. Louis, the train stopped at Sedalia, Missouri for breakfast, and a little time for a short stroll along the station platform.

As the conductor called, "Board," we clustered near the pullman platform to get aboard, and naturally awaited the lady passenger to mount the platform first. She was a lady of ample proportions and statuesque figure.

As she attempted to mount the first step it proved too difficult for her because her dress was of the then prevailing style, a hobble skirt, choked at the bottom, so that when she raised her foot to the high step, the skirt and the exposed black bloomers prevented her mounting.

Three of us gallant gentlemen sought to render aid; yet we failed, even after I had mounted the platform and took the lady's hands, while the two other gentlemen sought to push. Still no luck, until one man with brains as well as frustrated muscles rushed to the other end of the pullman, where the porter had his stool in his hand, ready to put it on the platform, as the train was just ready to pull out. Then he rushed back, and with a little help the hobbled lady stepped from the stool to the first step and reached the top just in time for her helpers to scramble aboard.

A Heartbreak at Dawn

At the dawn's early light, a young Negro boy and I stood on the platform of the M.K.&T. Railroad depot in our hometown of Hillsboro. I was waiting to board a northbound train for Dallas, and my companion was just waiting to see a train come in or by.

Up until that moment, he and I were total strangers, but it soon developed that there was a common bond between us. While we were still waiting for my northbound train, a southbound circus train came rushing by, bound for Waco, thirty miles away.

Until the caboose of the train passed, the boy stood in silent shock and disgust, and turning to me for sympathy, exclaimed, "Just going through little old Hillsboro. Just giving it the nuthin'."

From the beginning of time, as he and I reckoned time, a big circus had come to our hometown, just in time to harvest a big load of silver half dollars, during cotton-picking time. And now, to break a tradition and spoil a whole season, no stop would be made, and no boys would get up at 4 A.M. to see the circus train unload or tote water to the elephants. The big top would be set up thirty miles away. Times had changed for us.

She Reads Me

One of my real estate clients was owner and operator of a whiskey store. On one visit to his store to give him an opportunity to buy a good location for his business, I found him busy in his warehouse, loading a truck with his fire water, while a lady clerk was rearranging the bottles on the shelves.

As she had difficulty in reaching the higher shelves, I offered my services, for which she thanked me and said, "I bet you don't use this stuff." She was right. What a countenance?

A Puzzled Telegrapher

During World War II, my wife got word from her sister that her son (my namesake) had been shot down as he piloted a bomber over the war zone. We heard nothing for about a month, so did not know whether he was alive, dead, or in a German prison camp.

One day the lady at the telegraph station read a message

from Sister Lula, stating that Ernest was in a German prison camp. My wife, so relieved at knowing that he was alive, said, "Good. Thank you for your promptness."

In a minute or two, the lady called back and said, "Mrs. Thompson, did you understand that message?"

She replied, "I know it sounded strange, but we were so relieved to learn that the young man is still alive that it sounded good to me."

Puncture-Proof Tires

During a period in my life when I was appraising farms for a mortgage bank, a brother worked at the same institution I did, in the same mortgage bank, in an adjoining territory from mine.

It was the custom of the bank to sell land mortgages to some eastern investors, and allow them the privilege to reinspect the securities within a reasonable time, and if any were found to fail to meet the approval of the investor's inspector, the item would be rejected and settlement made.

One representative of an investor was the treasurer of a New Hampshire insurance company, who was a tight-fisted person, and was disposed to complain about any inconvenience which might be caused by making the inspection trips. And we soon learned that his knowledge of farm values was very limited.

After I had shown him a few items in my territory, I loaned my Ford roadster to my brother to show the man over his territory.

As they drove along, the guest asked my brother if his tires were in good shape, and was assured that they were. "My brother has puncture-proof tires. You can drive a nail into one and not get a flat."

They had not gone very far before something flipped by my brother's ear, and then another, and he discovered that my casings had grown so thin that the corklike stuffing had worked through, which meant a stop for a tire change. "The company should furnish proper equipment for their men," said the inspector, who was a constant complainer, and very stingy. We learned that the company had sent him on the road while his books were inspected, and he became a man without a job.

Dr. Davis Buys an Automobile

Dr. Davis had grown tired of feeding and grooming his horse, in addition to having to saddle him or hitch him to the buggy when a trip was required; so he decided that the time had come for him to improve on his mode of transportation by buying an automobile.

As my father, J. R. Thompson, was in the hardware and implement, buggy and wagon business, his store would be the logical place to go to buy anything in that line, including an automobile.

So, he and my father drew a catalogue from one of the pigeonholes in the roll-top desk, and read the descriptions and looked at the pictures of the various automobiles listed. An agreement was reached as to the item which was deemed suitable for the doctor's use, and the price agreed upon, and an order was promptly forwarded to the manufacturer.

Upon leaving the store, Dr. Davis demanded that he be allowed to uncrate and assemble the machine when it arrived. He did not want anyone else to touch it.

But when it did come, my father took the position that it would be his responsibility to deliver the automobile in proper condition, and that only a mechanic should be entrusted with that work. He considered that his man, Fred Grimes, was the man to do the job, for Fred was a good hand with any kind of machinery, and was assistant in the store's plumbing department, as well as a windmill expert. Another clerk was asked to assist Fred.

The machine was built along the lines of a buggy such as Dr. Davis used, having high wheels almost like buggy wheels, and was chain driven. It was a one seater.

Just as the boys finished putting this new buggy on its wheels, Dr. Davis drove by and asked, "What's that?"

"That is your new automobile, Dr. Davis," my father replied.

"No, it is not. I gave explicit instructions for no one to touch it, until I had myself taken it from the crate and assembled it."

Yet, after much discussion, and the dealer having explained that he could not let the machine be delivered without believing it in proper condition, as he would be held responsible to the buyer, and assuring him that Fred was a skilled mechanic, the doctor reluctantly took it.

That put my father out of the automobile business, as the doctor frequently visited when the outfit coughed or growled, and gave the house a dressing down for not obeying his instructions, which made the business unattractive.

I am not sure what year that happened, but it was about the year of 1903 or 1904, or within a year before or after those dates.

Fred Grimes became an institution, known to more people in Texas and many outside the state, than any other citizen of Hillsboro, as his signs reading, "Blank miles to Fred Grimes Garage, Hillsboro, Texas." He was a civic leader in the town. It was said that while Fred was in service in France, during World War I, a sign appeared: "4,000 miles to Grimes Garage, Hillsboro, Texas."

A Texas Delegation Visits President Wilson

Political-minded people will remember the long drawn-out session of the Democratic Convention at Baltimore, in the year 1912, which resulted in the nomination of Pres. Woodrow Wilson, after days of balloting, in the contest with Hon. Champ Clark, and other political leaders. To such people as do remember that contest, the excerpts from a letter from my lawyer friend, B. Y. Cummings of Dallas, will prove interesting.

When I was writing a history of the Farm Mortgage,

in the year 1947, I wanted help on a chapter dealing with the history of the Robertson insurance law, which had a profound influence on the development of mortgage lending in Texas. One of the most active leaders among the people seeking to pass the Gibson Bill, in 1915, to repeal the law, was my long-time friend, Hon. B. Y. Cummings, a Dallas attorney. As I was seeking information from the pros and the antis, I requested Mr. Cummings to tell his side of the story. It so happened that he had already written a twenty-six-page account of this battle, and in this story of his, he included a report of a trip to eastern cities by then Governor Ferguson and party, which tour included a visit to President Wilson. It reveals not only Mr. Wilson's character, but how it affected the men who had fought his nomination in the convention.

The following is a copy of that part of Mr. Cummings' letter dealing with the account of that visit.

In the autumn of 1915, the Governor received an invitation from President Woodrow Wilson to come to Washington, for the purpose of conferring with the President concerning the method to cope with the border disturbances, and the Governor accepted his invitation. He concluded to invite some of his friends to go with him on this journey and did so. . . .

The main object of the visit to Washington was a conference to be held between the President and the Governor pertaining to the existing border troubles between the U.S. and Mexico, and was, of course, to take place in privacy between the two men.

But it was also necessary, they thought, that the other members of the party should have an opportunity to pay their respects to the President of the United States. And, it was so arranged by Congressman Henry. Detailed instructions were given as to how the members of the party must conduct themselves in the White House. It is thought appropriate to repeat them here.

They were told that when they entered the building, to be at ease in the outer office until they were conducted into the presence of Mr. Wilson in his private office, where he would be seated at his desk. That there would be one vacant chair near the President, which would be used by the Governor when his friends retired. And, after a few words of greeting from the President, all should retire from the room except the Governor, who would remain for the conference which was the object of the visit.

The instructions were not followed literally, because some of them were cancelled by the President himself.

In view of what happened for the remainder of his life, his tragic illness; his worries and his death, it is pleasing to recall that on that December morning of 1915, he was in full possession of health, energy, intelligence and such personal charm as is possessed by few men in the world.

When the President arose, he was confronted by a group of visitors, few of whom had advocated his nomination for the Presidency in 1912. All of them stood stiffly at attention in a bona fide effort to obey the instructions which had been given for their conduct. Not one of them had been a member of the "immortal forty" at the Baltimore Convention and they were all sure that the President knew it. They also knew that the President felt profoundly grateful to the people of Texas for that long, continued support accorded him by the delegation from Texas, without which he knew he would never have been President of the United States.

Under the two-thirds rule, then in force, they had been able to force his nomination over the

Hon. Champ Clark of Missouri, who had commanded a majority at Baltimore through many long and weary ballots of that historic convention of the Democratic party. These guests of Governor Ferguson were therefore more or less ill at ease, because it was a political faction in Texas, who, in cooperation with William Jennings Bryan of Nebraska, had caused Woodrow Wilson to become President of the United States.

The President suavely and instantly relieved the tension of the moment. He expressed great satisfaction that the visitors had come. As best as can be recalled, he said he knew what restrictions had been placed upon them. He immediately ordered chairs for each of them. He told them that he felt under great obligation to them, but that often, in following the routine, he became quite lonesome. He placed his hand on the shoulders of each of them, and bade them wait until sufficient chairs arrived for the accommodation of them all.

We were entertained for a much longer time than was anticipated by any of us, and when, at last, we realized that all of his moments were golden, and that the time allotted for the conference with the Governor was being trespassed upon, we managed to withdraw.

Remembering how hard Mr. Cummings' group had fought against the nomination of Wilson at the convention, it was most gratifying for me to read this tribute to our then president, as I had been a staunch supporter of President Wilson from the beginning, having admired him for a long time after reading his *History of the American People.*

After Johnny Came Marching Home

The San Antonio of today is not the San Antonio

known to me. I would no doubt get lost if I now sought to drive through once familiar areas of that city of colorful history.

I have known two San Antonios, separated in point of time by a quarter of a century, and another forty years since my wife and I lived there, from 1923 to the year 1929.

The first San Antonio I knew was the one in the year 1895, when I, a pre-sophomore from college, spent my summer vacation at our home in the big colonial home at the north end of Main Street of Justice Denman, who was then living in Austin, and had rented the place to my father for the sum of thirty-five dollars per month.

Then we could hitch Shiloh to our surrey with the fringe on top, and drive slowly through the very narrow streets, and on out along the River Drive, now called Broadway. We could ride the streetcar to town, and to Travis Park Methodist Church on Sunday.

The other San Antonio we knew was not greatly different from the first one in customs and tempo of living. Instead of buggies and surreys, we travelled in automobiles, but could drive in a leisurely manner, visit the missions, and enjoy ambling at any speed we chose into the timbered hills. On Saturday night we could park in front of the Original Mexican Restaurant during the dinner hour, and then stop at the Palace or the Empire, and later, at the Aztec, for a view of a silent picture or to watch Don Felice walk majestically under the spotlight to take his place as leader of the Palace orchestra.

The giant bells of the nearby cathedral still boomed a message of a service or a funeral through my office window in the newly built Frost National Bank Building. At home, we could often hear the bugle calls from Fort Sam. All that we saw and heard gave us a feel of history, and a sense of easygoing living. One could relax by sitting for an hour in the lobby of the Gunter Hotel, the retired cowman's home at home or away from home, and enjoy the tales told by the red-faced old Trail Man, Ike T.

Pryor, and others. One could learn in what part of Texas could be found the best "cow ranch" section or the "steer country." We could enjoy a delicious Sunday dinner in a formal atmosphere at the Menger.

All of this quiet living gave little hint that for more than two hundred years, San Antonio had been headquarters for fighting men — Spanish, Mexicans and Americans, and that the most tragic of all battles had been fought there, except the visit to the historic Alamo.

Young Lt. Dwight Eisenhower and his bride began a career that led to a future undreamed of by them that year of 1917. Over the years there were enough gold bars to fill a nitch in Fort Knox, and enough stars to make a milky way. Many retired servicemen of all grades have found "Sunny San Antonio" a delightful place in which to retire.

But one week in the mid-1920s, a shock wave of soldiers, veterans of the first world war, returned to the city where many had learned soldiering at Camp Travis or in the nearby hills.

The American Legion was holding its long-heralded convention, which San Antonio leaders estimated would swell the population for the time being more than 100,000, a crowd that the hotels could not possibly handle; so homeowners were urged to make rooms available for the boys who had defended freedom.

But, though the crowd fell far short of the 100,000 visitors, the number who swarmed over the quiet city was sufficient to shock folks of quiet ways, like those of my good friend Watt Vaughan.

Though his work had of recent years put him in touch with city life, as he had his home there, his walk and his manner bespoke the farm from which he grew. The voice still had the resonance required as a manager of a Brazos Bottom Plantation, and any Negro who came from points east of the Colorado River immediately recognized in that drawl the voice of an understanding friend.

And, the pipe — one could not visualize Mr. Vaughan

without that pipe between his well-fitting, man-made teeth.

A rather slender figure of medium height, slightly stooped; a guileless man, an observer would say, who loved peace and meditation after the day's work is done.

As loyal people, Mr. and Mrs. Vaughan advised the proper committee, several months in advance, that one spare room in their modest home would be available if needed.

The weeks rolled by. The legionnaires came, not 100,000 strong, but in sufficient numbers to crowd the downtown hotels, boardinghouses and restaurants. The streets were thronged with singing, swaying men, under the influence of something more potent than the artesian water which San Antonio boasted in such abundance.

Several city blocks in the business center were roped off and dedicated to the visitors. No streetcars, busses or cars were allowed. Crap games on the street pavement, in front of its most central hotel, entertained great crowds of ex-servicemen, some with shirt tails in and some out. A policeman was defrocked and left standing in his underclothes.

And often in the day and night one heard the songs of the overseas men, the favorite being "Hinky, Dinky, Parley Vous," and the bugle calls split the air in due season. As the crowd of fighting men increased, a committee telephoned the Vaughan home and requested accommodations for three guests. "All right," said Mr. Vaughan. "If they are nice people and your committee will vouch for them, send them out."

The guests appeared — one man, his wife and his sister. The price of three dollars per day was agreed upon. "Oh, they were delighted to be in a home instead of down in those terribly crowded hotels."

There was a week of hilarity, with impressive parades during the day, with their continued singing and bugle calls. We civilians who sought our way to work and homeward had to detour several blocks morning and afternoon, and after a legionnaire's shirttail had been dunked into my coffee a few times, I abandoned my accustomed luncheon tables for some in the less popular districts.

"Well, Mr. Vaughan, how are you enjoying your guests?" I asked.

"All right, except that they stay out until two o'clock in the morning and sleep late, so I see very little of them. Mrs. Vaughan says the women seem very sociable. They come in to use the iron, and chat with my wife nearly every day."

"Where do they hail from?" I asked my wife.

"Somewhere in the North; Nebraska I think they said," she answered.

The eighth day came and the ex-servicemen were leaving, but Mr. Vaughan's guests had not gone. At the supper table, they consulted — Mr. and Mrs. Vaughan. "You know, Muz," he said, "I don't like the looks of things exactly."

"How is that, Dad?"

"Well, these folks claim they are from Nebraska, but they have a Texas license on their car."

"I noticed that," she said, "and I asked the ladies about it, and they said they had traded off their car in Amarillo."

"Well, they have been here a week and they have not said a word about paying their room rent. It is beginning to look suspicious to me."

Bedtime came, and Mrs. Vaughan suggested retiring. But Mr. Vaughan said, "You go on to bed. I think I will wait until our guests come home." With that he walked to his hand grip and took out his automatic, put it in his pocket, put his shotgun by the door, removed his shoes, filled his pipe, turned out the light, and sat near the door in his favorite chair. He settled himself for a long vigil.

"Dad, what are you going to do?" asked his wife.

"I am going to collect our rent from that Parley Vous bunch before any baggage leaves this house."

"Now, Dad, don't get into trouble over the room rent. Those seem to be nice people — guess they spent too much money, and maybe they are broke."

"Well, I have my idea about that bunch, and there will

be no trouble except my sitting up half the night."

"Now, you just go to sleep, and when you wake up in the morning, I'll have the room rent."

The sentinel dozed at his post. But none knew. There was no court martial, but the sentry let none by without the password.

About 2:00 A.M. a car came to a quiet stop at the corner of the block. It did not come into the driveway.

There were stealthy steps on the front porch. The voices of two women in whispered conversation came from the next room. Hand baggage came sliding out the door, as one man said to another, "I'll take these. You get the next load."

A man's footsteps were heard on the porch, when the sentinel, now full awake but unshod, stepped out on the porch. "Just hold on there. Lay those things down. Put them right back on the porch."

"What does this mean?" said the other man. "I have got nothing to do with you. What right have you to order me around? Haven't these folks paid their room rent?"

"Shut up," came the reply, and the plantation drawl had changed, and there was the quality of the machine gun. A plantation Negro would have known that the time for argument was over, and that the time for action and obedience had come.

"Tell that bird yonder to bring those grips right back here." And the light from the street lamp showed clearly the way the gun barrel pointed. The man came back, bearing only one suitcase. "Go back there and bring that other bag, and be quick about it," came the firm, clear command. "I am not going to waste much time with you bums."

Just then two frightened women appeared. "What's wrong?" Then, with sobs, one tendered her ring, if he would let them go.

"Keep your ring, sister, I don't want your jewelry," the host said.

"Now, you folks listen to this. You came to our home because we wanted to help San Antonio entertain the

Legion. Not for the money you gladly agreed to pay. We have treated you as ladies and gentlemen, which you are not, and trusted you for the measly amount of the room rent, instead of collecting in advance. Now if you bums, whether you are soldiers, camp followers, gamblers, or whatever you are, think for one minute you are going to get away with this, just try it, and you will go away in an ambulance."

"Mr. Vaughan, honestly, we are broke, and if you will let us go back to town, we can get some money from some friends."

"All right, but these women and this baggage stay until I am paid. This is a nice howdy do. I have to sit up until two o'clock in the morning to collect this room rent. Now, you two fellows can take your car and get the money, but don't come snooping around, thinking you can steal these women or baggage out, for this shotgun will be on duty all night."

The night wore on. The day came, as the two chastened night birds came, begging for an armistice. "If you will send the baggage C.O.D. to this address in Houston, we will get the money there and take it out."

"No, I will let you all go, and when you wire the money to me, I'll express the baggage to you. I am more dependable than you."

"I hope you will excuse me for being so late this morning," said Mr. Vaughan as he came to the office later than usual one morning, but I had to send that durn baggage off by express this morning. I got the wire from Houston. Durn that Polly Vous stuff."

A few years later I had my experience with well-oiled ex-soldier boys. I planned to inspect some farm land near Altus, Oklahoma, so my wife and I drove up there from Vernon, Texas one afternoon to hunt for a place to spend the night. The little Oklahoma town had only two very small hotels. One of them was full, so the clerk directed us to one nearby, but as we drove toward it, three weaving heroes came out with locked arms, in order to keep from falling, and a crowd seemed to exceed the capacity of the hotel, so we drove thirty miles back to Vernon, seeking sleeping quarters; then we got an early start the next morning back to Altus.

A week later, I had work to do in Corpus Christi, and found that another convention was in session there, but was able to find a room in the hotel; yet that did not assure me a night's sleep, for at 2:00 A.M. I was awakened by strident blasts from a bugle. The hotel was L-shaped, so that I could see into a room on my own level a flock of half-clads and no-clads, talking and singing, which continued far, far into the hours in which I wanted to sleep.

So, I searched the papers after that to see if Legionnaire conventions were scheduled for any of my ports of call.

The stories you have read are true, and no names have been changed, as I wanted to preserve the genuine quality of the subject matter, which could best be done by recording the facts, word for word, as they came from the lips of my good friend and fellow worker in the farm loan field.

Legal Lights on the "Forty Acres"

Four fine gentlemen, comprising the law faculty at The University of Texas during the spring months of 1906, when I sought instruction in that hall of learning, were not only able lawyers and teachers; each one was a unique individual with charm and a rich background of experience. All of them had been reared in a period of American history which encouraged young men to value the highest moral virtues and cherish the traditions of their forefathers.

Judge John Townes

My distinguished friend, Hon. Hines H. Baker, has condensed in a few words his impression as a student under Judge Townes. "Also, I had classes under Judge Townes who was the most challenging individual I knew on the faculty, a statesman and a lawyer founded in the fundamental principles." Referring to benefits of association with these fine men, Mr. Baker further says: "I could ramble a good while on my experiences under each of these professors, some of which were extremely amusing and much of which set standards for us to follow."

Judge Townes was of unpretentious manner, a staunch Baptist who was esteemed by everyone who knew him. The very fact that everyone knew of his strong moral character brought great amusement to the campus people when Mrs. Carrie Nation, after being told by the B. Hall boys of his intemperate behavior, caused quite a stir. This was brought out in that most interesting and delightful story of B. Hall, by Walter E. Long, which appeared in the *Southwestern Historical Quarterly* of April, 1959.

Judge B. D. Tarlton

It was my good fortune to have known Judge B. D. (Dudley) Tarlton, who was teaching real estate law. I knew him as a young lawyer during my childhood, in Hillsboro, and renewed my acquaintance with him during my short stay in The University of Texas. He was a man of aristocratic mien, a charming man, and a lawyer of distinction. A biographical sketch I hope will soon appear in a magazine. I hope it will do justice to this fine gentleman.

Again, a quotation from my friend, Hon. Hines H. Baker, condenses a picture of Judge Tarlton. "I suppose we had no more colorful man in Austin during the entire history of The University of Texas, and certainly no finer gentleman than Judge Tarlton."

It was my privilege to have classes under this fine professor for three years.

Col. W. S. Simpkins

The legends generated about the unique character of Colonel Simpkins, professor of law, in The University of Texas, are so well known to all old-time lawyers of Texas, that they would find little new that could be written about him, but there may be folks of the later generation who have not shared our memories of this colorful and celebrated character.

He was an ex-Confederate soldier and officer, who fired the first shot of the War Between the States, when, as a cadet lieutenant, in the University of the South, now known as the Citadel, he gave the order to fire on the Union gunboat, the *Star of the West,* a short time before the attack on Fort Sumpter.

With his long, wavy, blond hair and mustache, he reminded us all of the picture of Mark Twain.

When he came swinging his arms down the corridor of the law department, the junior Laws, on hearing him coming, set up a welcome by stomping, clapping hands and beating the desks with law books until the colonel was seated. He glowered at us, though evidently pleased.

He relished uttering cryptic remarks on any occasion which might bring a laugh, such as: "What struck you? A thought? I am glad to hear someone ask questions in this class. It is evidence of dawning intelligence . . ."

After telling his class about the Roman Ambassador of Goodwill, Sperygrinus, one of the class undertook the job of creating a portrait of the animal described as "Perigrinoose," which soon became the generic title of all lawyers. The colonel approved it and told how it had the qualities of a lawyer.

Judge Miller

I regret that, as a junior Law, and a part-time middle Law, I did not have the opportunity to have classes under the then dean, Judge Miller. But his appearance, and from his occasional talk to the Laws, he impressed me as a quiet and thorough man of good figure, and one who deserved and received the respect of everyone who knew him.

I left lots of legal knowledge at the university, as I took little away, but I carried portraits of the beautiful campus and its dignified buildings, and the many colorful characters who appeared on the scene when the scholastic population was one thousand, all individuals who lived in an atmosphere where loyalty was born.

Texas Weather

I have been exposed to more weather than the average person for two reasons: I have lived longer than many, and the first seventy years of my life were spent, for the most part, out of doors, sometimes in vigorous work. The last twenty years has made me "chicken," along with air-conditioning, and reduced mileage of travel.

Some of the weather manifestations best remembered by me include the following:

In about the year 1884 or 1885, the thermometer at our home registered four degrees above zero, which affected us much more than it would now because the houses were floored with one pine floor, and the houses were from twelve inches to eighteen inches above ground, allowing the cold winds to cool us from every side and bottom, too.

Other impressive dates were the cold winter of 1895; the record breaker of 1898-1899, cold, drought, heat and rain; 1912, hot summer; 1917-1918, winter cold; 1929, and 1930, when the Dallas record was three degrees below one year and three degrees above the other.

But the year that only old folks can remember was the record-breaking winter of 1898-1899, and the spring and summer of 1899. I felt the full force of every hot and cold, wet and dry day of that period.

The Record Snowfall, about January, 1899

Although I can spot the February date when our home thermometer registered sixteen degrees below zero, and an unofficial record keeper in Fort Worth showed ten degrees below for that area, the exact date of the big snow that fell about two or three weeks before then cannot be pin-pointed, but every other detail is etched on my memory.

All day long that cold day the gray clouds were drifting south over us. I was ploughing with a three-disc plow, six-mule team, thinking at the end of each long lane that I might be forced to take out, but as no rain came, I kept going, until I noticed the lead mules' ears pointed toward the northwest, where a black cylinder-shaped cloud came rolling toward us. It almost touched the ground.

As quickly as I could, I unhitched the team and started them in a lope toward the barn, a mile away. With the lines tied and thrown over my shoulder, I was able to keep up with them, as the snowflakes, each the size of a half dollar, began to cover the ground. By the time we reached the barn, the ground was white, and the little herd of cattle came up the lane from the pasture, bawling; it was the first time for weeks that they had been to the barn lot.

Our sheds were in a small lot, where we put the horses, mules and milk cow. Around it was a much larger enclosure we called the "Run around," enclosing the machinery sheds, granary, and feed bins and strawstacks. Here the cattle gathered, to eat the kafir and sorghum we spread for them, as they huddled behind stacks and buildings.

The next morning we saw snow two feet deep over all the level wheat fields, and up to one's armpits in the ditches and along the fence rows. We needed to go to town, but could not travel some of the roads, so we drove through the neighbor's pastures where the land was rolling, and snow not so deep.

There was a railroad cut near the water tank, on the Fort Worth and Denver Railroad near Chillicothe, three miles away, which was so deep in snow that a snow plow from Denver was sent down to open the cut, we were told.

If I am permitted to write another weather story, I will tell about the February blizzard that really broke the record with twenty-two degrees below zero at Dalhart, and the windswept wheat fields of the spring and the man-killing heat and rains of summer.

The Galveston Storm

Most Texans are familiar with the effects wrought by

the terrible September 1900 storm, which swept over Galveston with such destructive force and killed as many as six thousand or more people.

It will impress one with the size of Texas, when I relate just how little I knew about the storm when it was raging and the weather conditions in the region of Chillicothe, Texas, in the southeastern fringe of the Pan Handle, and then to hear the story from the colorful Shanghai Pierce of Matagorda County, describing the damage done in his area.

On a very hot day in early September, 1900, my brother and I were loading wheat in a freight car at Chillicothe, Texas, to ship to Galveston for storage, to await what we hoped would be a better market.

All that hot afternoon, we had sweated and worked, scooping wheat from the wagons into the freight car and just about 5:00 P.M., the car was closed and we were ready to seal it, so it could be picked up by the next southbound freight train, when we received a telegram from our father who lived in Hillsboro which read: "DON'T SHIP WHEAT. GALVESTON BLOWN AWAY." We had to unload it all.

We relied upon the *Dallas Semi-Weekly News* for keeping us informed with the world outside, and had heard nothing of the storm until we got that wire.

Not only Galveston, but the whole area along that part of the Gulf Coast suffered, and the big pasture man and farmer suffered great damage, as explained in one or more of his letters quoted in that most entertaining book by my long-time friend, Chris Emmett, entitled *Shanghai Pierce*. And since during his serious illness, he sent me word to use any part of his book I desired, I am at liberty to quote parts of Shanghai's various letters to bankers and others touching on the effects of that dreadful storm.

Pierce was a unique character who would make a mountain out of a two-bit item in trade, and at times proved one of the most generous men anywhere. He had friends, and he had enemies, but the story of his life is never dull.

On the 16th of September, the Colonel came out of the house, after the so-called Galveston storm had struck down everything on the Texas coast, and devastated the country for hundreds of miles inland. He looked about, and quietly said, "I have turned rice boomer. I see Borden's crop has stood the storm without damage, when everything else is blown to atoms." Then he went back in the house, and penned a personal note to D. T. Beals, President of Union National Bank at Kansas City, asking that $80,000 be sent to his nephew, G. G. Guiford, to be used for the relief of Wharton County people, through his bank. "The terrible calamity," he wrote, "which has just befallen our county, in which we were in the middle, has caused the need of money. The people are wrecked and instead of having money to deposit, they are bound to draw out every dollar they have. Wire me as soon as you receive this." Then he drew his check in favor of C. D. Kemp for $1,103.00 to tide him over his misfortune, and said, "Friend Kemp: We got pretty badly torn up here, but my Galveston loss was perfectly enormous, and, Kemp, you and two other men are the only men that could get a dollar from me now."

Next, the Colonel turned his thoughts to G. G. Williams, President of the Chemical National Bank of New York, who had so readily come to the rescue when Weeks, McCarthy and Co. was in trouble. Chuckling, he said, "I have old man Williams of the Chemical in good humor, and will try to keep him so." Then he wrote:

"September 23, 1900, Mr. G. G. Williams, Chemical National Bank, New York City, New York.

"As you have seen the full accounts of the fearful ordeal we have just passed through, and are no doubt somewhat worried in regard to it — if

you will have a listen to my tale of woe, I think
I can satisfy you so that you will lose no sleep
as to my indebtedness to your bank, but in our
present condition it takes patience and oodles
of it; firstly, we have been nearly swept from the
face of the earth, and at least 8,000 people have
gone from this world to God only knows to
what port they land at. Here, at my ranches, I
was badly torn up. Many houses, barns, feed
houses ended flat to the ground, and I have built
a very nice little church for my people, all at my
own expense, and the Good Lord saw fit to give
it a H — of a lick, and nearly wrecked it.

"So, my first thing is to replace my buildings
and my windmills, of which I have dozens, to
water my stock; all of which are more or less
wrecked; many entirely gone. We have had ex-
cessive rains, and overflows ever since March, until the storm; more rain has fallen than we had
in any one year in the last forty-eight years,
which had damaged my crop very much, and to
cap the climax, the storm swept the entire crop
from the face of the earth.

"The crop on my convict plantation, 1800 acres
in cultivation alone, would have been worth
$30,000, and the worst of all, I have one hundred
Negroes on my plantation, east of Colorado River,
which I am bound to take care of until August,
and at least one hundred German and Bohemian
farmers to whom I have sold land that can't pay
their Int. nor notes maturing, but I will get every
dollar of my money and interest by being lenient.

. . .

"Galveston was rotten as Sodom, and I think
that is one cause of the Lord's visiting in with His
wrath. I will enclose you a round schedule of my
assets, in which there is no wind or water, if let
alone. The storm covered an area of about one

hundred miles wide. My nephew and private secretary has been very sick and is at Hot Springs, and on his return, if you desire, I can give you an exact statement.

"Now, Mr. Williams, rest easy, and I will pay you every cent I owe you and Int. and I ask no sympathy, as sympathy is collateral for nothing, but do ask this of you. When you have your board of directors together, state them my case fully, and ask them when I have paid you every dollar of principal due you that they give me a rebate of two per cent, making my interest four per cent instead of six per cent. And, if the Lord, in making them, finished his job and put a soul in them, then they will do it without a word. If you will give them a solid talk, one thing you bear in mind there is no liens of any kind against any of my property, and my credit in Texas, good as it ever was. Forgive me for this long letter, and would be pleased to hear from you. I am yours truly, A. H. Pierce.

"P.S. It takes a barrel of money to run my business. Don't fail to give your board that talk about reduction of interest of 2%, which no doubt the Lord will give them two per cent credit in Heaven. The Good Lord knows they are going to need it."

When Shanghai opened his mail at his B. U. Ranch, he found a letter from an old time friend who wanted to pay his indebtedness by delivering some personal property, all that was left to him after the devasting storm. Pierce declined to accept it; writing encouragement instead. "You will make a good crop next year, and need them, so don't get discouraged."

In the same vein, he addressed a letter to one of his own army captains, J. K. White, who offered to sell everything he had and pay the receipts over to Pierce, as a credit on his overdue accounts. "Captain. No. Just go ahead and fix up your houses. I will carry you over another year. We will make a crop someday, and we will come out all O.K. The storm nearly wiped me off the face of the earth, but we must trust in Providence, if the breaching breaks. Very Res. your old friend, A. H. Pierce."

In addition to my recollections of the 1900 storm in Galveston, I recall others that impressed me very much.

1915 Hurricane

When the 1915 storm hit the Texas coast, we were living in Hillsboro, and after reading the *Dallas News'* account of the hurricane, we observed a line of buttermilk clouds bordering the horizon. I hurried to get in the car and head east to make a land inspection ten miles out, as I felt sure that before nightfall we would feel the effects of the storm. My wife and I had just time to get back in the house before noon, when the wind came with such force that the rain fell like sleet, horizontally, and a day or two after that the green cotton stalks looked as though a killing frost had hit them.

1919 Hurricane

We were still living in Hillsboro when this storm hit the Corpus area, in September, and though I do not remember whether the deluge of rains we had fall occurred at that date, so much rain fell that the cotton in the bottom fields was nearly shoulder high, and the leaves so dense that the bolls would not open. They would have rotted had not the leaf worms hit them, and let the sunshine in which saved a big crop.

A few years ago, when I sought information for a story of a lady who lived in Beeville, she wrote me a full account of how that 1919 storm hit Corpus Christi, and brought on pneumonia to her father, Judge B. D. Tarlton, which caused his death.

She, with her children and father and mother, were in the Nueces Hotel, which faced the bay in Corpus Christi, before any seawall was built. The lower floor was filled with water, much damage was done, and they were marooned. The family suffered much discomfort in their trip back home to Beeville — a tragic story.

When we moved to San Antonio, and my field work made it necessary for me to work in the Corpus Christi area, I saw great slabs of concrete sticking out all along the area of a former causeway that once had been. The people below the bluff suffered greatly. But, when I visited the mansion of Mr. Joseph Green, manager of the Taft Ranch, situated on the bluff near the bay, or the Gulf, I was told by Mrs. Green that though the spray from the water had reached their third floor, no real damage was done.

1933 Hurricane

I think the year was 1933 when the hurricane hit the Rio Grande Valley so hard. I was stopping in Corpus Christi, when the storm started, and drove to San Antonio, to get on higher ground before the full force of the wind hit the coast.

Two of my field men were in the hotel in Edinburg when the storm hit, and for two days I could not reach them by wire or telephone, and the whole valley was like a lake.

When they reported, they said the roof of the hotel was blown off, and their windows blown in, and when at the end of the second day, as they started home, the water was a foot deep on the highways.

Since coming to Houston thirty-five years ago, we have had some dark days and nights, but no great damage except near the water's edge, although the streets were lined with tree limbs, and we had no lights for some time.

Copy of a reprint of my story published in the October 1963 issue of the *Southwestern Historical Quarterly* at The University of Texas.

Melvin A. Traylor, 1878-1934[1]

When the little coal burner, with its mixed train, came to a stop at the lonely Cotton Belt depot, in Hillsboro, Texas, on that December night, in 1898, a heavy rain was falling. The depot marked the end of the forty-mile stretch of rails leading from the Cotton Belt Main Line at Corsicana to Hillsboro. The line, which served five little towns between its terminals, was known as the Hillsboro Tap. The cheerful whistle no longer floats across the black prairies, for the Tap is no more. It served its time in the days of dirt roads and horse and buggy travel.

Among the passengers was a young man of twenty, with a whipcord frame and a cheap suit of clothes, Melvin A. Traylor. When the conductor told him the day coach would not be used until the return trip the next morning, he got permission to sleep in it that night. He did not know it then, but he had reached the halfway mark between his humble beginning and leadership of men. Twenty years before that night he lay in a cradle in a log cabin home in the mountains of Kentucky. Less than twenty years later, he would, as a Chicago banker, stand before six hundred bankers of the Seventh Federal Reserve District in Chicago and call their attention to the fact that men were dying in Flanders Field, and that foot dragging must stop, for the United States government needed funds to carry on the war. His reward would be rousing applause and oversubscription of the quota for Liberty Loan Bonds.

Three states have a right to be proud of Melvin Tray-

---

[1] The writer acknowledges gratefully help extended by many persons — from Texas town to financial marts. Melvin's widow, Dorothy Traylor; his son, Melvin A. Traylor, Jr.; and his brother, George Traylor; the boards of trustees of Northwestern University and of Berea College; James B. Forgan, Herbert Hoover, and Joe B. Frantz have all added to the fund of information.

lor. Although a Kentucky farm was his birthplace, Texas was his training ground for a career of which he did not dream when he ended that long, wearisome journey to Texas in December, 1898. Illinois was the arena of his greatest accomplishments as a financial leader of the nation before his death, at the age of fifty-six.

My association with Melvin A. Traylor gave me a close insight into his character and his work, for Hillsboro was my home where I was employed by a subsidiary farm loan bank to the First National Bank of which he was president. Although I knew him during the last thirty years of his life, which ended in February, 1934, I have found twenty-seven years later, during my research, that he had covered fields I knew not of, and his stature was even greater than I had imagined.

Too many men, in every decade of our history, have risen from humble beginnings to leadership in business and professions to warrant another biography unless the subject's record was exceptional. Traylor's record was exceptional; his successes resulted from a combination of stern self-discipline, hard work, and economy of time, as well as of friendliness, honesty, and modesty. From the use of these qualities and attributes he also acquired a cultured personality without the aid of any advanced schooling.

What he accomplished, he did without the aid of wealthy friends, speculative ventures, or extreme forceful-ness, for his friends and associates pushed him into places of leadership which demanded his abilities. Frazier Hunt recounted the story of Traylor's life in most eloquent terms on a radio broadcast in 1931 sponsored by the New York Life Insurance Company. Hunt declared that it was a story of real drama — American drama.

Forty miles from the birthplace of Abraham Lincoln, James and Kitty Traylor lived in a log cabin on a one-hundred-acre farm near Breeding in Adair County, Kentucky, not far from the Tennessee border. Their forebears had come to the region over the Wilderness Road through the Cumberland Gap from Tidewater, Virginia, and the

Shenandoah Valley. They were of sturdy, self-reliant stock, mostly Scotch-Irish and English, seeking freedom from the restraints of the older settlements and the ownership of land. The Traylors were Methodists and Democrats.

On October 21, 1878, their first child was born. For the first twenty years of his life, Melvin Traylor called the log cabin home. He received such instruction as could be had in a country school that was open five months in the year. He learned the meaning of hard work by doing chores at home when he was small. As his strength and stature grew, he worked on the farm and in the country store at twenty-five cents a day to help his father support a growing family, as six other children came to his home.

Melvin had one advantage over Abe Lincoln in that he had the influence of a happy, well-ordered home, where the main book was the family Bible, where honesty, courage, and self-denial were taught, and where ambition was encouraged. Although life was simple, and luxuries nonexistent, the family's daily needs were supplied, and the verities of life instilled.

As ambition moved him to action, he rode over to the county seat where he studied for a teacher's certificate, and at the same time studied Blackstone's commentaries, which he had borrowed from an ex-Confederate officer who was a prominent lawyer in the community. When he obtained his teacher's certificate, he took a job as a teacher in the Leatherwood Creek school, at a salary of thirty dollars a month for a five-month period. He still worked after hours in a store.

In school he had been active as a debater; therefore, when a preacher began campaigning for William McKinley, the local Democrats put up Melvin to champion William Jennings Bryan in the strenuous campaign of 1896. There were no neutrals in that year following the panic of 1892 when prices for farm products were depressingly low. Free coinage of silver at the ratio of sixteen to one, or adherence to the gold standard were the issues of the day.

Two years later, at the age of twenty, Traylor became restless and decided to heed the suggestion of friends and relatives who had moved to Texas to try his luck there. He rode his pony to the county seat, fifteen miles away, then took a stage over the thirty miles to Campbellsville, where he boarded the first train he had ever ridden. His trip took him to Hillsboro, Texas.

Melvin's move did not make any sudden advance in his fortunes. Instead, he started at the same level as in his home section, as a clerk in George Patterson's grocery store, at a salary of twenty dollars a month. To save two dollars a week room rent, he joined the fire company, which gave him a place to sleep free. He was a fire fighter for seven years, the last two years as chief. His picture in uniform now hangs in the city hall, which also housed the fire department. To pay his board, he took a job as night clerk in a hotel where he worked from seven o'clock until eleven o'clock in the evening.

He arranged to leave the store at 3:00 P.M. after working from daylight, so that he could either attend Patterson Institute or study law in a lawyer's office. Nelson Phillips, the young lawyer who was probably his mentor, later became chief justice of Texas' Supreme Court.

Among his store duties was the driving of the delivery wagon, and the late Olin Culberson, former railroad commissioner of Texas, recalled seeing Melvin driving to Patterson's Institute behind two little Spanish mules.

In 1901, Traylor was elected city clerk and was admitted to the bar. He became assistant county attorney of Hill County in 1904, and when the political wheel turned him out of office, he opened his own law office. One year's work convinced him that financial success was a long way off in the legal profession in a small farming community, where there was a strong bar composed of lawyers in their prime of life and where clients were farmers or merchants of modest means and few legal problems.

To the surprise of his friends, he walked into the Citizens National Bank one day and told Oliver G. Bowman, the executive officer, that he was quitting the law profession and wanted to learn the banking business. When Bowman told him that the bank had no job for him, he said, "I don't want any money, but I want to learn the business." The banker thought such a man deserved a try and put him on the books. As a result of this bold move at a time when jobs and salaries were at a great premium, Melvin convinced the bankers of his ability and self-reliance. They sent him to the town of Malone which had a population of 150, to operate a small bank owned by the directors of the Citizens National. There, he was a triple threat, playing at every position: banker, janitor, and night watchman. He put a cot between the desk and the vault in the bank and slept there at night.

Soon his ambition found another spur toward the goal of success. He was married to a charming young lady of one of Hillsboro's fine families, Dorothy Yerby, who was to share his struggles and his successes, and who still lives in Winnetka, Illinois.

Each move he had made in life had broadened his experience and helped him in dealing with men of every character. When he arrived in Hillsboro, he had found that a large segment of the population both in the town and in the surrounding country were from the southern states and that Tennessee and his own native Kentucky were well represented by many of the leading men in the community. In addition, there were enough northern people to fill the post office jobs during a Republican administration. At Malone he had found many people of German descent. This association proved helpful to him when he later moved to St. Louis and Chicago, where people of that nationality were active in every line of work.

As a growing boy, on the Kentucky farm, Melvin had lived through the panic which began in 1892. While he was an apprentice banker, the short-lived 1907 panic taught him human nature and diplomacy, for this was really not so much a credit panic as it was a currency panic. No one, bankers included, wanted to part with a five dollar bill for fear that it would not be replaced. This caused the tellers to induce a man who presented a check for payment to accept a deposit slip, assuring him that his checks would be honored. The banker knew that many of these checks would drift in to be deposited by merchants or others. A short panic in 1914 and a serious one in 1920-1921 taught him that prices did not run on one-way streets.

In January, 1908, Traylor accepted a position as vice-president of the Citizens National Bank of Ballinger, Texas. In 1909, the Citizens National Bank and the First National Bank of Ballinger were consolidated as the First National Bank, and he was made president, a position which he held until 1911, when he was offered a job with the Stock Yards National Bank of East St. Louis.

His work among the virile, enterprising people of West Texas added further to Traylor's fund of valuable experience in dealing with the public, for there he found men who had the pioneer spirit and courage, cattlemen as well as farmers. The opportunity to make loans on livestock as a representative of the banks and commission houses of St. Louis, Kansas City, and Chicago proved a valuable part of his education for greater responsibilities. In the St. Louis bank, he expanded the operations he had begun in West Texas.[2]

In 1913, Traylor was offered a vice-presidency of the Live Stock Exchange National Bank of Chicago, and the presidency of the Chicago Cattle Loan Company.

By 1918, James B. Forgan, a canny Scot who was a powerful figure in financial circles and chairman of the board of the First National Bank of Chicago, had deemed it imperative to offer Traylor the vice-presidency of the First Trust and Savings Bank.

Forgan's appraisal of Traylor is shown in his book

---

2 A personal knowledge of Melvin A. Traylor's life has been supplemented from *Melvin A. Traylor, Homespun American* (Fort Worth, 1932); Berea (Kentucky) *Citizen*, October 1, 1931; *Northwestern Alumni* (November, 1934); Dorothy Traylor to W. E. T., July 26, 1961.

Recollections of a Busy Life, which explains how valuable Traylor's services were to all financial circles.

I knew that Mr. Traylor had previously been offered two or three important official positions in large New York Banks. He had also very successfully and patriotically organized for the Federal Reserve Bank of Chicago, through banks of Illinois, an agency for the wider distribution of Government war issue bonds and notes. The Board of Directors of the Federal Reserve Bank, of which I was then a member, had selected him for this gratuitous service, and so well satisfied were they with the way he handled it that they had decided to ask him to enter the bank's service permanently, as Deputy Governor. As I had him in mind already for the other position, I took no part in the proposition before the Federal Reserve Bank directors of securing him for that bank. The suggestion, however, accelerated my action, and I promptly put the matter before our executive committee, and secured its unanimous consent to offer him the presidency of the First Trust and Savings Bank.[3]

In 1919, Traylor became vice-president of the First National Bank of Chicago, and in 1925, he became its president, a job which would appear to have been sufficient to tax the ability of the best of men, though it was but one of his many positions. In 1926, he was elected president of the American Bankers Association, having previously served as president of the Illinois Bankers Association. Traylor was also elected president of the American Golf Association in 1928. Golfing stars such as the immortal Bobby Jones still remember and highly esteem Melvin Traylor. His interests ranged even more widely as shown

---

[3] James B. Forgan, *Recollections of a Busy Life* (New York, 1924), 155-156.

by his presidency of Shedd Aquarium and his membership in the Chicago Art Institute and the American Economic Association. In 1929, Melvin became a member of the organizational committee of the International Bank of Settlements, in Basel, Switzerland. He was for twelve years a trustee of Northwestern University, serving as president of the board for the last two years of that period. He was also a trustee of Berea College in Kentucky and of the Newberry Library in Chicago. The resolutions passed by the trustees of these colleges and letters from officers are most impressive in their praise of Traylor.

Only people mature enough to have lived and been in business in the years of booms and depressions can understand the problems which faced businessmen and bankers. He rode the boom of World War I, and saw the collapse of the cattle, cotton, wheat, and other markets in the sudden drop in 1920 and 1921. He saw with foreboding and warning, the expansion of realty and stock prices through the middle and late twenties, and had to face the long night of the depression in 1929 and in the 1930s. That was truly the time that tried men's souls. He stopped a run on his own bank, helped the Reconstruction Finance Corporation and other banking institutions keep open the Dawes Bank, whose closing might have brought down the walls of financial structures all over the Chicago area, and perhaps all over the country. He worked hard with Jesse Jones to put the banking institutions in Detroit back in operating condition. He helped the schoolteachers in Chicago get their long-overdue salary payments.

The true picture of Melvin A. Traylor cannot be seen, however, by merely looking at the work he did or the positions he held. The vast scope of his capacity can only be measured by a full study of his career and by reading his many speeches made to bankers and chambers of commerce, which reveal a cultural development and a clarity of expression, a philosophy and a spiritual quality with deep roots in love of his fellowman. He once told his son, "Remember, your friends are your most valued possessions."

129

During the depression, Traylor returned to Hillsboro for a brief visit. Anyone who talked with him, as I did, in front of Smith-Tomlinson's hardware store and saw that he was the same warm-hearted, democratic fellow as the fire chief he had been twenty years before, would know then that he was more than a successful banker. He was a real man.

Only a man of exceptional character and capacity could call forth eulogies from B. C. Forbes, from university presidents, from boards of trustees of colleges, and from radio speakers like Frazier Hunt. Melvin A. Traylor gave his life to his fellowman through the development of a capacity for service by the use of the sterling qualities of thrift, self-discipline, courage, self-denial, hard work, and a friendly spirit, most of which are reflected in his speeches. Such a life was made possible by the era in which he lived, when the thirty-hour week was unknown, and no man was penalized for doing more work than his quota allowed.

Melvin Traylor never sought great riches. He tried to do his best on any job assigned him. The real breadth of the man is reflected in what Walter Dill Scott, president of Northwestern University, said on October 15, 1934, a few months after Traylor's death.

> Among the many outstanding characteristics of Mr. Melvin A. Traylor, the one that has impressed me most was his catholicity of interest. This was clearly demonstrated in his relationship with Northwestern University. He was never disturbed by minor details, but saw all problems in their broader relationships. To him Northwestern University was an institution exercising many functions; all of which were important, and to all of which he was willing to give his undivided interest and efforts.[3]

---

[3] Florence Stewart to W. E. T., May 1, 1961. This letter from the Archivist of Northwestern University includes a copy of the text of Scott's speech.

An excerpt from a speech which Traylor made to the American Bankers Association in Houston on October 25, 1927, gives some insight into his character and his thinking.

> This, then is my hope for our future; that we may be rich without forgetting to be righteous; that we may be powerful without being offensively proud; that we may be nationally minded without being narrow minded, and finally, that we may live in a world of fact without surrendering our faith.[4]

The closing words of Frazier Hunt in his radio broadcast from New York, after interviewing Traylor, in 1931, also are well worth quoting.

> I am wondering if the character and integrity and common sense that this man drew from those backwoods, Kentucky hills of his, and that humble, but fine, deep-rooted home has not been more valuable than all the garnishment of formal education and formal knowledge could possibly have been.
>
> You can't teach courage and character in schools and colleges. They are born in homes and fields and streams and woods. Without these two virtues Melvin Traylor might have become somewhat of a figure in the banking world, but would not have been the leader of a new conception of the duties and obligations of our great business and financial men.
>
> His is an American story, of American opportunity, and of American character and courage.

Friends and loyal employees waited anxiously through his long illness, hoping each day would bring improvement, but one day in February, 1934, Melvin A. Traylor

---

⁴ *Melvin A. Traylor, Homespun American,* 21.

131

yielded to the ravages of pneumonia and exhaustion at the age of fifty-six. His life had been a strong thread in the fabric of American history. If he lacked the color of eccentricity, it was offset by a rare consistency such as few men have, based upon a proper appraisal of the value of time and orderly planning so that every hour might count for growth in knowledge, culture, and usefulness. As Frazier Hunt said, "Here is real drama, American Drama."

The Man to Match His Mountain

When writing the foregoing story, it was necessary for the author to use restraint in order to condense the telling in order to find a place in a historical magazine which had two or three years' supply of material on hand, and also, to meet the approval of the scholarly director, Dr. H. Bailey Carroll.

Yet the stature of a man like Melvin Traylor could not be measured by a thumbnail sketch. A person blessed with dynamic vigor, combined with self-discipline, and broad and expanding horizons, could not be fully understood nor appreciated without further knowledge of his activities and the scope of his work and human relations.

So, I am asking the indulgence of the reader while I supplement the foregoing sketch, which was first published ten years ago, and I will submit additional information by further research and by telling the story of the author's close personal relations with Mr. Traylor, and his attitude toward a friend and to every employee of his great institution.

New material has been discovered which told how he was always ready to be helpful to everyone with whom he came in contact.

With the permission of Mr. John T. Jones, owner of the *Houston Chronicle,* and an official of the Jesse Jones Foundation, I am permitted to quote parts of Mr. Jesse Jones' story, in *Fifty Billion Dollars,* relating some of his work he did with Melvin Traylor. This will be followed

by reports from a few celebrated golf champions, who tell
of Traylor's helpful assistance in their behalf.

Mr. Jesse Jones Works with Traylor

In his book *Fifty Billion Dollars*, Mr. Jesse Jones gives
a dramatic and interesting account of the steps taken by
the Chicago banks, the R.F.C. and the New York banks,
federal reserve banks and the U.S. Treasury, and President
Hoover. I have borrowed a small section of that report to
show how influential Melvin A. Traylor was during some
most trying times.

Mr. John T. Jones, nephew of Mr. Jesse Jones, and
manager of the Jones Foundation, has given me permission
to quote from *Fifty Billion Dollars* in my Traylor story.
Some excerpts follow:

> On the morning of Saturday, June 25, ten days
> after the General left us, I arrived in Chicago, as a
> delegate to the 1932 Democratic Convention, which
> was to convene there the following Monday. This
> was the convention that nominated Franklin D.
> Roosevelt for his first term as President.
>
> From my hotel that ominous Saturday morning,
> I walked through the Loop, and watched the tail
> end of the week's terrible run on the big down-
> town banks. Thousands of frantic rumor-spreading
> depositors were still milling about every bank
> entrance in LaSalle, Clark, and Dearborn streets.
>
> Bank lobbies swarmed with nervous customers.
> Many of these disturbed people had already lost
> heavily, in the collapse of outlying neighborhood
> banks, which had dotted almost the entire city.
> Others, during the two previous months had seen
> part of their savings disappear when the Insull
> empire "a Customer ownership public utilities"
> crashed into insolvent splinters. Furthermore, dur-
> ing the previous three weeks, twenty-five of
> Chicago's outlying banks had closed.

On the Wednesday preceding my arrival, the bank run fever had spread into the Loop, where Chicago's five big banks were located. Among these being the two largest in the Middle West, the First National and the Continental Illinois. On Thursday, the Carroll chain of seven banks had failed to open. On Friday, eight more of the smaller corner banks were piled up into the week's wreckage. Alarming rumors fanned the fears of the city's millions, of whom hundreds of thousands, being unemployed, had only their dwindling savings on which to exist, and could not afford to lose their deposits or have them tied up.

At eleven o'clock that Saturday morning, Melvin A. Traylor, the chief executive officer of the First National Bank, breasted the wave of fearful depositors sweeping through his banking house. Stepping up on the pedestal of a marble pillar, in the savings department, he calmly addressed the crowd.

He said he did not blame them for worrying or for what they were doing after all that had happened to the banking business in Cook County, but he wished to assure them that if they would talk to people who knew the facts, they would learn that the First National, which had been in business 70 years, was sound, and in a position to pay all its depositors their money. Mr. Traylor was regarded as a possible Presidential nominee of the Democratic convention that was to open its sessions two days later. He was placed in nomination by the Illinois delegation.

Saturday night, General Dawes, whose bank had seen its deposits slip, within a year, from $240,000,000 to half that amount, made a decision, which, he later explained to one of his friends, so relieved his anxious mind that, for the first time in the ten nights since he returned to Chicago, he was able to get several hours of untroubled sleep. His decision was not to open his bank on Monday morning.

He arose very early on Sunday, and assembled in his office his principal associates and also a few leading officials of the other larger banks.

Mr. Traylor, after his first conversation with General Dawes, got in touch with Edward Eagle Brown, the executive vice-president of the First National, and asked him to call other officials of the First National to a second meeting in their bank. He told Mr. Brown, that in his opinion, the General meant what he said about not opening Monday.

Later that morning, Mr. Traylor came to my hotel room, and asked me to go with him to a meeting of bankers. He did not tell me the purpose of the meeting, or where it was to be held, but his demeanor manifested that it was serious and urgent. He took me to the Central Republic. We got there a little before noon. Gathered in the Board room were thirty or forty of Chicago's leading bankers, businessmen and industrialists. It was obvious that they had been waiting our arrival, and that I was to be, as the saying goes, the fall guy.

GENERAL DAWES DECIDES TO CLOSE HIS BANK

Quietly, but with a firm jaw, and an attitude that carried conviction, General Dawes told us that he had called the meeting to inform the other banks in Chicago, and me, as a Government official, that he did not intend to open his bank the following morning, Monday. He gave as his reason that while he thought his bank was solvent, the "smart money" was being withdrawn through the clearing house, as well as over the counter, at the rate of more than two million dollars a day, and he did not intend to sit idly by and allow frightened depositors to get all the ready cash the bank had available to meet current demands, while friendly, trusting depositors, and those who were not in the know, might be forced to wait for their money until the bank could be liquidated. He made it clear that he was not asking for assistance, but he said he wanted to inform the other banks of his purpose not to open his bank, so that they might take such steps as they could to meet their own requirements, when his bank did not open the following morning.

It must have been apparent to all those present, as it certainly was to me, that renewal or continuation of the bank runs and clearing house withdrawals would force all the banks in the Chicago area to close. The General was the coolest man in the room. The situation was dramatic in the extreme.

We sent out for sandwiches, peeled off our coats, and got down quickly to the business of seeing what could be done. It was nearly sixteen hours later, just before Monday's dawn, that we put on our coats again and left the bank to go to bed.

After Seventy-Two Years

During the last thirty years of Melvin Traylor's life, I knew him, and during that time formed a lasting friendship. During the succeeding forty years I have done considerable research from year to year in order to confirm or add to my knowledge of Melvin Traylor. From my files, and from my memory, I shall try to portray the man as I knew him.

Esteemed by Bobby Jones

Although a "duffer" in golf, Traylor was made President of the American Golf Association. In response to my letter to Mr. Robert T. Jones, Jr. (known as Bobby), Mr. Jones expressed his high regard for Traylor, as shown by a few quotes:

I have a tremendous admiration for him and deep affection, as well. He was so thoroughly honest and down to earth in every thought and action.

Mel was a man of sound good sense. He had a deep humility despite a calm assurance, which gave us all so much confidence in his judgment and advice.

Caddies to College

Through the several letters received by me from two golf champions, during the 1960s, I learned a most interesting story. Mr. Charles Evans (known as Chick Evans) received an invitation to join the Northwestern University "N" Club forty years after he attended another University (Chicago University); and Chick Evans and his friend, and fellow golfer, got Melvin Traylor to launch a foundation for sending worthy caddies to college. Through correspondence with Mr. George H. Hartman, vice-president of the advertising firm of MacManus, John & Adams, Inc., and his friend, Charles (Chick) Evans, Jr., who were golf champions a long time ago in Northwestern University, and now associated with the same advertisement firm, most interesting details are revealed, and I will now condense the story.

Chick Evans and his mother had for years sought to start a fund for aiding worthy caddies in getting a college education; but Chick said it looked like it was going out, instead of up, until they, with the aid of Mr. Hartman, induced Mr. Melvin A. Traylor to help. This resulted in his taking funds from the Western Golf Association as a starter, and got the foundation off to a good start, so that at the time of our letter exchanges, five hundred boys were attending college, and a thousand or more were alumni and now holding positions of high rank in many institutions.

Mr. Evans' mother took note that the president of the Western Golf Association was also a trustee of Northwestern University and made contacts. Mr. Evans was most emphatic in stating that Mr. Traylor was responsible for getting the foundation off the ground and into a going concern.

College Team of Limited Means

In a letter addressed to me, dated November 1969, Mr. George H. Hartman told me how, in 1921, he met Mr. Traylor at the Midlothian Country Club, of which Traylor was president. Hartman was that day a member of a team in Chicago University which won a championship game at the club course. Traylor was present and was an enthusiastic booster for his club. Later, he got the club to invite the team members to full use of the club's facilities, knowing that as many were working their way through college, they could not afford the cost of membership.

Traylor Warns of
Impending Stock Market Fall

Mr. Hartman tells of his attending a luncheon of businessmen in 1929, three weeks before the October disaster in the stock market. "One thought of his I will never forget. He said he wished he could talk to every man in this great country of ours and beg them to stop gambling.

"Never did I see Mr. Traylor so worried and impressive in telling us what he thought," said Mr. Hartman.

Jim Farley Writes

In response to my letter of February 10, 1965, Mr. James A. Farley, former big wheel in the Roosevelt administration, and former postmaster general, responded on February 23, 1965, in which he states: "Mr. Traylor was an outstanding American, and would have made an excellent President if he had been nominated and elected, because everyone who knew him had a high regard for him personally, and for his ability."

Esteemed by University and
College Board of Trustees

For twelve years, Mr. Traylor served as a member of the Board of Trustees of Northwestern University, and during his last two years on the board, he served as president.

On February 24, 1934, Bishop George Craig Stewart, speaking for the committee of three members of the Board of Trustees of Northwestern University in offering a resolution of respect at a memorial service, condensed in one paragraph, among others, a portrait of the man who had served the university:

> Melvin Traylor was to us a brother beloved, a tried and intimate friend. We knew him, admired him, trusted him, loved him. He brought to every task a rare combination of intellectual capacity, social charm, and moral strength. He combined utter honesty with business shrewdness, courtesy and dominant leadership; consideration with power, gentleness and cheery friendliness, with intensity of deep conviction and unswerving purpose.

> Rich in saving common sense,
> And, as only the greatest are,
> in his simplicity sublime.

A Trustee of Berea College

Mr. Traylor did not forget the friends of his childhood, in the Kentucky mountains, and served for several years as a member and as president of the Board of Trustees of Berea College, and resolutions expressed views similar to those most eloquent memorial resolutions offered by Bishop Stewart of Northwestern University Board.

A Message to the Kentucky Legislature

During the years of 1931 and early 1932, friends of

Melvin Traylor in Texas and Kentucky sought to start a campaign to nominate him on the Democratic ticket for president of the United States, and an exhaustive biography of Mr. Traylor was circularized in his behalf, but, he did not aspire to hold any political office. During this period he received an invitation from the Kentucky legislature to address them, which he accepted.

He stressed two ideas especially. One was that there was a need for reducing federal taxes, and among the ways to do that was to curb federal spending and subsidies to one and all. He said, "Federal aid is a seductive fallacy. It seems to dull the senses, and lull to sleep the pride in local self-government, and the joy of independence which characterized our forefathers.

"Unless we are willing to surrender to the federal bureaucracy the independence of thought and action, we must reverse our course of action."

No Political Ambition

Because his friends in Texas and Kentucky were urging him to throw his hat in the ring, he expressed genuine appreciation for the honor bestowed on him by this compliment, but added:

> I confess to having been something of a daydreamer, but I can honestly say that in my most brilliant excursions into the world of "What Might Be," I have never included the romance of high political office. No normal American could other than be pleased that his friends should think of him in such terms. I am grateful but I have not been, nor am I now, and do not expect to become a candidate for political office.

Traylor Shocks the Members of the International Chamber of Commerce

On May 5, 1931, Melvin Traylor addressed the members of the International Chamber of Commerce, where a thousand men, from thirty-five countries, heard him score the business leaders of the country, and especially the bankers, for encouraging speculation.

He told them of the evidence of the approach of trouble as early as 1927. He charged that with mergers and stock splitting, it was made too easy for little people to speculate and that actions of Wall Street were plain crap shooting.

In the November issue of the *American Magazine,* Jerome Beaty tells an interesting story illustrating the viewpoint of one of the listeners.

A white-haired old gentleman in broadcloth who had arrived at the convention after the speaker had been introduced, leaned toward his neighbor and indignantly said, "Who is that fellow, and who let him in here, and what does he know about the integrity of financial leadership?"

His neighbor, a youngster of forty-five, grinned, "That fellow? That fellow is one of the western boys that you easterners maybe never heard about, but, Mister, you are hearing now, and how."

"Traylor who?" the old gentleman scoffed, and trying feebly to be funny, added, "Traylor Horn?"

"Mister Mel Traylor from Kentucky and Texas; now president of Chicago . . . maybe, Mister, you never heard of the First National of Chicago either."

The old gentleman's eyes opened wide. Now, he remembered. "Well," he breathed, "that is that fellow," and quickly he cleaned his eye glasses and inspected the speaker as one for the first time, gazed on a strange and dangerous animal from a far-off land.

In response to my request, former Pres. Herbert Hoover had his Traylor files searched and sent me, with

141

other copies of items from his collection, a full copy of that address that had been given him. The title was "The Human Element in Crises."

The Man I Knew

I had so many sources of information about the character, habits and goals of Melvin A. Traylor it would be impossible for them to be recorded in a readable space. Material from each avenue confirmed the impression one would receive from another.

Many days were spent in company of the ranking officers of the First National Bank of Chicago. I read letters from the postmistress of Malone, Texas, who knew him there, and from a young lady cousin who said he offered help in her schooling. Letters from his son, Melvin, Jr., confirmed the opinion I held. I knew his wife, who, as a widow, furnished data to help. Melvin Traylor's letter to his mother, dated thirty years after the day he arrived in Hillsboro, threw light on the subject. *The Recollections of a Busy Life,* by the veteran chairman of the board of the First National Bank of Chicago, told how he had been observing Mr. Traylor, as a man who got things done and hired him to prevent his going to New York banks, or to the Federal Reserve system, where offers were extended.

As we were almost the same age, and had struggled through the same conditions in the same atmosphere, there was a bond of sympathy that created an understanding of each other so helpful in creating an image.

I really began knowing Traylor about the year 1901, when I was working as chief clerk in a real estate and farm loan office in Hillsboro, and he was just beginning his professional career as a lawyer, which lasted only a short time, because he realized that a young lawyer with limited schooling and training would find it a long pull to meet the competition of men of the Hillsboro bar, who were in their prime and enjoyed fine reputations, and, taken all in all, during that period, a small town had limited earnings.

In my overstuffed files, I have hundreds of letters, articles, and pictures, including letters from his widow, his brother, his son, and bankers from all over the country.

One quality that Mr. Traylor had beyond the capacity of any other person I have known was an ability for proper use and planning of his time, a commodity we all have, but so few of us spend it wisely. He made every hour count toward a definite goal, yet had time for warm friendship, which never seemed to interfere with his other plans.

The scope of Melvin Traylor's work and influence was not fully realized by me until long after his death in 1934, because years and years of diligent research brought to light records of the vast amount of work he did, and the good he did, as his horizons expanded, offering greater opportunities to his use of mental, moral and cultural growth.

But before all these additional facts were learned and stored in a Traylor file, I had learned to know the man who made such a record and this acquaintance ripened into a lasting loyal friendship that never diminished and never ended.

Beginning as acquaintances in 1901, with a common heritage of home lives which encouraged thrift, honor, industry, and where ambition was encouraged, we shared our young manhood in a small town, where separate dreams were born and nurtured. Although separated for many years, each of us was aware of the other's stepstones in the business world.

Then, one October day in 1915, as I sat in the lobby of the Morrison Hotel, in Chicago, Melvin Traylor came into the lobby and found me, and took me to the manager's desk for a credit endorsement. Then we chatted about our work and the old times. Then, our relationship as acquaintances grew into that of friendship, which lasted through good times and bad, as I later found work in the Texas subsidiary of the First National Bank of Chicago, of which he had then become president. It is about this man, as a man and as a friend, I wish to talk now, the man who his close friends knew, too. Traylor's proper management and use of time (which we all have to use) made his record possible, as each hour was assigned to an allotted task.

Only a law student of that day could appreciate the amount of concentrated thought and time required to dig through Gladstone's philosophic discussion of the English common law by a beginner before he ever had a chance to study Texas statutes or Texas cases. He did that while working from daylight until 3:00 P.M. as a twenty-dollar-a-month grocery clerk, being available to put out fires, and acting as night clerk until midnight.

Fortunately, the extent of legal knowledge then required to get a license to practice law was less than now, and the examination was made by a committee of local lawyers who gave an oral examination on the fundamentals, and usually approved the granting of a license. But, he found work as assistant county attorney shortly before he decided to "learn the banking business."

Melvin Traylor was the most democratic man I have ever known, meaning in the broad sense. He had the happy faculty of adapting himself and his attitude to the environment, without ever losing the ring of sincerity in his voice or in his purpose.

Traylor could command the attention, the respect, and the affection of the leading businessmen of America, with the same ease he commanded fellowship, the admiration and the love of the small-town man with whom he worked in humble capacity.

I have stood with him on the streets of Hillsboro, and seen the smile that accompanied his handclasp when he met some old-timer with whom he had served in the fire department thirty years before. And, I observed that it was not a Chicago banker that they rallied to welcome to the hometown, but rather it was Melvin Traylor of old.

I have seen him in business circles where tact and courage and business capacity were demanded to hold his own. And he manifested the same frankness, the same

cheerful smile of confidence that won over the big businessmen as well as the small ones.

I have ridden with him for hours in a car alone, and
the word *I* seldom came into the conversation. He had
a prodigious memory for names and faces, which, of
course, was taxed by reason of the fact that, as head of
the American Bankers Association, he was called upon to
recognize scant acquaintances from every part of the nation.

As a leader, he inspired the loyalty of his lieutenants,
because he placed confidence in them and their integrity
and in their ability to accomplish the work assigned them;
he did not hamper them with detailed instructions. If they
succeeded, they got the credit. If the results were unsatis-
factory, after they had done their best, there came no
reproof.

In a busy life, I have occasion to have heavy correspondence with business and professional men, and I have never
yet found a correspondent equal to Melvin Traylor. He
had the happy quality of saying exactly the right thing,
in a short letter, without brusqueness or metallic quality.

Although his business responsibility covered a much
wider field than being president of one of America's largest
banks, and despite the fact that he worked longer hours
than any other executive officer, he always appeared un-
hurried to any visitor to his office.

In addition to his duties connected with his own bank,
he served as active director on many corporate boards;
among them were the Standard Oil Company, and the
S.P. Railroad and the many other activities heretofore
discussed.

Melvin was truly a great man. He took the talents the
Lord gave him and developed them to their greatest capacity. His is a record that no lazy man could have at-
tained, and no small man could approach. He was such
a many-sided man that he seemed a composite man, embracing the virtues of many strong men. We, who have
worked with him for years and years, could find no sub-
stitute for him.

We in the Dallas office daily awaited reports from

Chicago while our leader fought the ravages of pneumonia, until the word came that the career of a gallant man had ended: *The Man to Match His Mountains.*

Introduction to the Story of Attorney General, James Stephen Hogg

One may ask, "Why the story of Governor Hogg?" His record is so familiar to the people of Texas that one may deem it but a repetition of well-known facts.

The author's motive for this undertaking is due to his effort to write a chain of stories about the men who have served Texas as attorney general. But, there is an added factor which motivates this sketch. When James Stephen Hogg was conducting his campaign for re-election as governor of Texas for a second term, my father, J. R. Thompson, Sr., was chairman of the Hill County Hogg for Governor Club, when I was a half-grown boy. This made me deeply interested in Mr. Hogg, who was a well-known public figure.

For the important facts in his life story, I have depended upon the short, but most interesting, biography written by Dr. Robert C. Cotner,[1] and by reading the speeches which were embraced in the same volume. Yet much of the history, nature and character of the political conditions of the contemporaries of Governor Hogg were firmly fixed in my mind. I hope this sketch may be accurate and create the sort of portrait as I see this man and his family which is so important in the story of our state. *I was there.*

James Stephen Hogg

"There were giants in those days," the days in which James Stephen Hogg grew to manhood and assumed a leading role in the political and economic life of Texas. To understand a man, one should know the social atmosphere he breathed, and the type of men who set the

---

1 Dr. Robert C. Cotner has given me written permission to quote some essential items from his book.

pace for public life and the problems he was called upon to solve.

Statesmen

Sen. John H. Reagan was Hogg's neighbor, a man who had served as a member of the cabinet of the Confederacy, and sought to bring peace and law to the exhausted South. Others were Judge Orem M. Roberts (the Old Alcalde), who taught the young hopefuls the principles of law; Gen. Lawrence Sul Ross, who protected the frontier, and became the head of the A&M College; the Honorable Horace Chilton, senator and conservative leader, highly respected by all. There was the stalwart Richard Coke, Judge Alexander Terrell, and Attorney M. M. Crane, statesmen, all. There were orators like Joseph Weldon Bailey, a contemporary.

Political and Economic Climate

This was the era of railroad building. They were piercing the forested land of East Texas, and spreading over the prairies of Central Texas, North Texas, and West Texas. Railroad tycoons like Jay Gould and C. P. Huntington wielded sweeping power, a power which grew into danger of monopoly and allied evils.

There was the birth of the Grange, the spread of the populist party doctrine, which now seems modest as measured by the moves and aspirations of today's Democratic party into transmutation of The Great Society.

It included the period of the Republican party of the Reconstruction Era, known as the black republicans, and its evolution into a party seeking to adapt itself to realistic conditions, and later dividing into two factions, the Lily Whites and the Black and Tans, which in course of time saw clashing between lumberman Lyons and railroad man E. H. R. Green.

During the 1890s, Grover Cleveland, the Conservative Democrat, served his second term; William Jennings Bryan, the golden-voiced orator of the Platte, electrified the Democratic Convention in Chicago, and swept the party into the Free Silver Column. Many "Sound Money" Democrats, called "Gold Bugs," supported the Republican nominee, William McKinley.

In the closing days of the nineteenth century, Teddy Roosevelt, who put the fire and color into Colonel Wood's Rough Riders, charged up San Juan Hill, and started the United States of America on her crusade of world power, which was later to embrace islands of the Pacific in the U.S.A.

Along with these colorful personalities came, too, the West Texas droughts, with covered wagons going west, and returning east. The young folks sang such songs as "After the Ball Is Over," "She's Only a Girl in a Gilded Cage," "Dazie," and "A Bicycle Built for Two." And some called it the Gay Nineties. But the men whose cotton crop brought only four to five cents a pound, and the wheat raisers, after battling dry weather and dangers of cyclones, had to sell their wheat for thirty-five cents did not find it so gay.

During these years immigration swept people from the older states into Texas, over the newly laid rails, laying out little towns that clung to the rails to keep from being sunk in the mud or covered by sand.

Enter James Stephen Hogg

Into this period of Texas history came a real giant, both in body and mind. His name was James Stephen Hogg, whose family furnished leaders for a longer period of time than any other one family, beginning in the year 1839 when Col. Joseph Lewis Hogg, father of James Stephen, moved to Nacogdoches, Texas, and extending to this year of our Lord, 1973. Each generation gave the state leaders of stature and philanthropic actions that helped preserve the cultural and educational institutions of Texas, and is still bringing cultural influences to the community under the leadership of a great lady, Miss Ima Hogg, a daughter

of the late James Stephen Hogg, and who is affectionately
known as "Miss Ima" by people high and low.

James Stephen Hogg, son of Col. Joseph Lee Hogg and
Mrs. Lucinda McMath Hogg, was born at Mountain Home,
near Rusk, Texas, on March 24, 1851. His father, brigadier
general in the Confederate army, died in Corinth, Mississippi in 1862. James was left an orphan at an early age,
and worked as a printer and editor of papers in various
Texas towns; he was elected justice of the peace, county
commissioner, district attorney, attorney general of Texas,
and governor.

After retiring from political office, he resumed the
practice of law, and made investments which laid the foundation of a fortune. He died in 1906. Thus we learned of the
beginning and the end of the life of a great man, and the
titles of the jobs he held. This is often all the history
known of most of us.

James married Miss Sally Stinson, at her home in
Gilmore, April 22, 1874. The following year, he was admitted to the bar. His father-in-law was a scientific farmer and
horticulturist, a granger and large-scale lumber operator.
He discussed with James the discriminations, rebates and
other abuses of railways toward farmers and lumbermen.

From the year 1873 to 1884 he was a public officeholder
except for two years. James Hogg rapidly acquired a reputation for the economical administration of public funds.
An honest and vigorous law enforcement officer, he helped
clean up northeast Texas, just as his brothers, Judge Tom
Hogg of Denton, and Sheriff John Hogg of Decatur, were
doing in the area northwest of Dallas.

Within a period of thirty months he reduced the floating debt of Wood County from twenty thousand dollars to
one thousand dollars and reduced the taxes from seventy-five
cents on the one hundred dollars to twenty-five cents, which
he states was "all done by law, under the law and according
to the law, without impairing the rights of any individual,
or abridging the necessary public demands."

After retiring from the governorship in 1895, James
Hogg entered again into the practice of law and in making

investments that laid a foundation for the family fortune which has been used by him and his children for the benefit of all people of Texas. He helped organize the Hogg-Swyane Oil Company shortly after the coming-in of the Spindletop Oil Field.

He suffered injuries in a railroad wreck and spent much time resting in his handsome brick home on the Varner Plantation in Brazoria County. He died in 1906.

The above recital gives some idea of the general story of his life. Let us now consider the following:

Political and Social Atmosphere

It is reasonable to believe that the Lord tailored James Stephen Hogg for a special service to the state at the time he reached his maturity that equipped him for the responsibility. Let us consider the conditions which contributed to his entry into the race for attorney general and to his later election as governor.

Mr. Hogg was the first native son to become governor. Up until his election as attorney general, two forces were leading factors in the political arena.

The people of the South, including Texas, honored the leaders of their "Lost Cause." These men had not only served the South so gallantly, but were reaching an age to be at the peak of their powers; hence they had been so often supported in their quest for office that the ex-Confederates were a strong force on election date.

Another group, which naturally embraced many ex-Confederates, were the East Texas political leaders. That part of Texas was peopled by the old and earlier stock than the prairies of Central, North and West Texas.

After Mr. Hogg had demonstrated his ability to get every lesser job done in the most effective manner, when he was assigned one, some of his friends advocated putting younger men in office, and at the same time the politicians in East Texas took note of the fact that men of vigor had ambitions and leadership other than those in the area around Huntsville, Tyler, Palestine, and other older towns.

The East Texas men decided that in order to avoid losing their leadership, some strong, young, and courageous leaders should be put forward as candidates for state offices.

Mr. Hogg not only qualified in that way, but he advocated many progressive measures, and the enforcement of some laws that had not been used. He agreed with his old mentor, Sen. John H. Reagan, that Texas should have a railroad commission to guard against the exploitation of the Texas people by the railroad tycoons, notably Jay Gould and C. P. Huntington. These worthies had been manipulating the stocks of some lines to enrich the owners of the dominant lines by loading the small lines with bonds and then letting the roads rust away.

Wildcat insurance companies needed curbing or to be put out of existence.

The big range men and big pasture men, too, had become so powerful in West Texas and other range areas that a demand by the small cow man or farmer made the office seeker give thought to his position on such vital questions. Hogg did not hesitate to let his attitude be known on every paramount issue. Let us now consider how he dealt with each as the problem became acute. Like other attorney generals, Hogg inherited some knotty problems from his predecessor.

The Judge Willis Ouster Case

One of the first battles the new attorney general inherited from Attorney General Templeton was the prosecution of the case involving the ouster of Judge Frank Willis of the Panhandle area, in which his decisions had nullified the state's control of the range lands by dismissing cases or by permitting men, such as the powerful old cattleman Charles Goodnight, to sit on the jury and act on cases involving the cost of rental of the range land from the state lands. The Land Board sought to collect eight cents an acre for leased land, but Goodnight and the other big range men wanted to hold the fee to four cents, and wanted to do away with the Land Board.

The lower house voted the removal of Judge Willis but the Senate did not approve it, so the new attorney general learned how difficult it was for an official to control some local conditions, when the people of such a sparsely settled area did not want the controls, and who took the position that a man from East Texas did not understand the conditions in the western part of the state.

Curbing Wildcat Insurance Companies

The battles involving Attorney General Hogg were so often continued into the period of his administration as governor that this discussion will often deal with his work as with one continuous administration, for in addition to his efforts to enforce existing laws while he was acting as attorney general, he often drafted laws to be enforced while he was either acting as the state's attorney or as its governor.

It became necessary for him to challenge the right of many insurance companies to operate in Texas. Some of these companies had their headquarters in the state, and many had their offices out of the state. Life insurance ethics had not been developed to any great degree in those days and it has been asserted that Mr. Hogg's vigorous prosecution of ouster cases saved the people of Texas a great deal of money.

Hogg's Stand on Prohibition

In seeking office, Hogg had opposed the passage of a prohibition act, asserting that he believed in temperance but not in prohibition. His speech on this subject is one of the soundest and sanest expressions on that side of the issue that I have heard, and I was opposed to his views even then when I was a child.

The Law Must Stand Between
Two Forces of Extreme Views

In Mr. Hogg's campaign speeches, he described the

theories and practices of two classes of society who sought to control the trends and the destinies of the country.

On the one extreme is an organized class whose purpose is to remodel society by regulating property on new theories, limiting the modes of industry and prescribing the sources of livelihood, and changing the domestic relations and governing the morals of mankind.

The first has for its weapon the terror of force, propelled by inflamed passions, under the guidance of distempered reason.

On the other hand is a federation of voracious individuals, whose insatiate avarice leads them on to feast indiscriminately upon the vital substances of every class within their way, without the comfort or welfare of society at all.

This second holds in its grasp the power of wealth as its means of triumph. The former means destruction by blunt coercion. The later intends it by insidious absorption.

Subject to the incursions of both is the great conservative class, who compose the Republic's life. However, in command of it, for use in defense of aggression to protect the cherished institutions of our government, from wreck and ruin, by the collision of these two contending extremes, is the Law. Let it impartially, yet unyielding prevail. . . .

Throughout all of Mr. Hogg's speeches is the stress put on the demand for the rule of law.

Railroad Stock and Bond Law

Attorney General Hogg made a vigorous fight against the stock watering of bonds, with which the railroads and other public corporations had been mortgaged for more than their worth. This action on the attorney general's part led to a strict supervision of each issue before it could be offered on the market, in order for the investors to be protected, and for the railroads to keep from being thrown into bankruptcy.

The County and Municipal Bond Law

In order to curb the same loose and illegal issuance of watered municipal and county bonds, his attention was centered on such matters which control gave not only to the communities bonded, but strengthened the market for the bonds, as none could be issued without the approval of the attorney general's department.

Hogg Advocates the Creation of a Railroad Commission

In order to effect a needed control, Mr. Hogg urged the creation of a Railroad Commission, so long advocated by his old friend and mentor, Sen. John H. Reagan. This involved the state in a long contest. For even after the legislature created the commission, it took time to get the court's approval of its constitutionality. So, its power to control was postponed.

This support for the creation of the Railroad Commission, and for the enlargement of its powers, and for appointment to membership, instead of being an elective office, created one of the most determined fights on both sides of the question in our political history.

As governor, the first commission formed was by his appointment of John H. Reagan, who had resigned from his position as U.S. senator, to become the first chairman of the commission. He was the logical man for it as he had not only been urging its formation for some time, but he had the mental and moral qualities to do the job.

Opposing these measures were not only the railroads, but many businessmen who believed it would create a restraint on investors who might otherwise invest money in Texas.

One of the most active leaders in this opposition was

Judge George Clark of Waco, who was later to run for governor against Hogg. They believed that the laissez-faire, or former status quo, was the safest course.

But, Mr. Hogg was strong in his determination to bring the control of the railroads and other corporations to the courts and laws of Texas. The first Railroad Commission was composed of Senator Reagan, W. P. McLean, and L. L. Foster.

Mr. Hogg, with the aid of some able lawyers, checked the proposed law to eliminate amendments which would have weakened it or made it subject to court rejection.

Hogg and Reagan so strongly urged the creation of this Railroad Commission because there was a need to correct the conditions brought about by the manipulations of railroad controls, stock watering, and monopolistic gobbling up of competing lines, which let them gather rust while the big trunk lines fattened on profits of high freight and passenger rates.

Among the leading actors in this unsavory drama were Jay Gould and C. P. Huntington, controlling figures in the Texas and Pacific and the Southern Pacific lines, respectively.

These "worthies" had brought about a formation of a "Traffic Association" with the expressed intention of preventing discrimination, but in effect, according to Dr. Cotner, became a powerful pool to exact a rate tariff as high as the traffic would bear.

These tycoons issued their orders from points on the eastern seaboard and St. Louis, where their headquarters were located. Hogg determined to have Texas railroads with headquarters in Texas.

Alien Land Law

The British and other foreign investors became holders of large ranches and other tracts of land which Hogg deemed would be detrimental to the welfare of Texas; so he encouraged the passage of a law forbidding foreign individuals or corporations from owning lands in the state, and requiring them to liquidate within a given number of years.

Mortgage Lenders

As Scottish and British-American mortgage companies became quite active in making farm and ranch loans here, it meant that in cases of foreclosure, they would become fee owners; so the law made provisions for requiring the liquidation of such lands in a reasonable time. The year 1889 seemed to be one of the most active years for the chartering of such new companies in Texas; this happened during Mr. Hogg's term as attorney general.

As I spent forty or more years in the farm loan work, and sometimes represented such companies, I am quite familiar with the history of their operations.

Laws Against Perpetuities and Corporate Ownership of Lands

In order to prevent huge corporate ownership of Texas lands and control of land, which would be detrimental and ownership to the small land and home owner, Hogg championed the passage of law restraining such corporations and their holding lands in corporate names.

A Champion of States Rights

Governor Hogg repeatedly protested the invasion of the rights of the state by the president. He feared for the future of our democratic form of government if such trends were not checked.

Although he admired President Cleveland, and was loyal to his democratic chief, he criticized him severely for his having sent federal troops into Illinois to suppress the Pullman Company strike, which the president did on the grounds that the U.S. mails must go through. But, Hogg claimed that it was not done at the request of the local authorities nor of the governor of Illinois.

He Warned of the Hazards of Accepting Monetary Aid, Gifts or Subsidies From Washington

Hogg urged the rejection of the bounty to sugar raisers,

including the sugar raised on the state's farms, because to yield on one item would lead to further acceptance grants, and with each, a series of curbs and restrictions would follow. He expressed his views as follows, in part.

Mr. Hogg deplored the frequent use of injunctions by the federal courts in railroad cases, and cited the danger growing out of the trend of the courts to extend their powers which he deemed were unauthorized by the Constitution. He quotes Thomas Jefferson on that point. "We have seen that contrary to all correct examples, they, [federal judges] are in the habit of going out of the question before them, to throw anchors ahead, and grapple a further hold for the future advances of power. . . . They are then, in effect, a corps of sappers and miners, steadily working to undermine the independent rights of the States, and to consolidate all of the power in the hands of that government in which they have such an important freehold estate."

Hogg Advocated Restricting the Tenure of Judges

Hogg was in harmony with the declaration of the demands of the Democratic party for the reduction of the tenure of U.S. judges to less than life.

Citizen Hogg Extends His Great Service to Texas Beyond His Official Life

Governor Hogg's contribution to the welfare of his state did not end with his holding of public offices, for he then launched a movement that has been of unmeasured benefit to the political heritage by active service, as a leading citizen, and by building a substantial fortune, which was dedicated to the benefit of mankind. His support of educational institutions, and by giving to the state four children who took up the torch greatly increased the financial benefits to many worthy causes.

In a railroad wreck he was injured and his health impaired. In order to try to protect his health, he retired to his beautiful Varner Plantation home, near West Columbia. In time, oil interest in Spindletop and other fields laid the foundation of a great fortune.

The Governor Hogg as He Appears to Me

In reviewing the picture which I have of one of Texas' great men, I feel that his greatness cannot be measured by his political activities only, but by the depth of his understanding of the paramount virtues of his fellowman, his breadth and tolerance of their weaknesses, and his courageous support of the fundamental principles which should govern men and nations.

In Conclusion

Whether or not one believes there is eternal life after "we shuffle off this mortal coil" depends upon faith and the deep feelings in the souls of men, that their spirits should not die nor their work be lost.

Yet, as to our earthly survival, we have evidence all around us that the life one lives can be extended far into the future. Today, the image of Jim Hogg, in all his great height and massive frame and mind, is still before us, and by reading his honest, fearless, lucid speeches, we may read his thoughts. By looking around The University of Texas campus, and seeing the monuments and schools all over this state provided by him and his family, we know that his spirit goes marching on.

The Saga of Torpedo 8

Preface

On the fourteenth day of May, 1968, I visited in the home of Mrs. George Gay and returned her treasured scrapbook, with magazines, papers and books which she had graciously loaned me. These treasured items, which told over and over again the story of her son's dramatic part in the historic battle of Midway, were most helpful to me in my effort to recount the Saga of Torpedo 8.

Mrs. Gay is the widow of my long-time friend, the late George H. Gay, Sr., and she is the mother of George H. Gay, Jr., one time Ensign Gay, of the U.S. Navy Air Force, who was the only survivor of the ill-fated squadron, Torpedo 8, which flew from the flight deck of the carrier *Hornet*, on the fourth day of June, 1942, as it attacked the Japanese fleet.

Included in about thirty books and periodicals which Mrs. Gay allowed me to read were current newspapers, magazines and books. Two books were specially helpful: *A Ship to Remember* by Alexander R. Griffin, and the *Incredible Victory* by Walter Lord, and the newspaper series of stories in *Graphic*, by Loyd Wendt and the hero, George Gay, in the issue of May 18, 1948 and subsequent issues. Also, the *Saturday Evening Post* had a thorough recital later on. But, the *Incredible Victory* was written after a quarter of a century allowed for research and interviews with the actors in this drama.

Mr. Lord has completed a most thorough review of the entire Midway campaign, and Mr. Griffin, in *A Ship to Remember*, has given a colorful description of the carrier *Hornet* and her crew and her fighting men. So, I am indebted to so many writers, that I can only say it has been my hope to absorb enough to write a brief sketch of the operations, with special emphasis on the daring operations of Torpedo 8, and the part which my friend's son played in this historic battle.

I told Mrs. Gay good-bye as she was preparing to go to New York to visit her son Captain Gay during his vacation period. Then, she loaned me the new book by Mr. Lord.

The story of Ensign Gay's part in this historic battle has been clearly fixed in my mind for the past twenty-six years, but I wanted to try to absorb the whole story before attempting to present it to those who do not remember it.

There are many other stories to be found in a review of this battle: tales of the defense of Midway by the men stationed there, stories of the fighters and bombers from the

Hornet, the *Enterprise*, and the *Yorktown*, and army men, as well as the navy.

You Will Never Be a Pilot

"You will never be a pilot," the medical officer told George H. Gay, Jr., after he submitted his second application to enter the army aviation service.

That discouraging message was heard by George Gay about twenty-eight years ago, before he had enlisted in the navy, and was also commissioned ensign, in October 1941. Since he heard that opinion of the army doctor he served on the carrier *Hornet*, and joined his buddies in the attack on the Japanese navy, and saw twenty-nine of his shipmates and fifteen planes fall in the sea, in the fiery battle of Midway.

Now, in June 1968, the same Ensign Gay, now Capt. George H. Gay, is piloting T.W.A. planes from New York overseas. I wonder if the captain himself knows how many flying hours have passed since he was deemed unfit to be a pilot? I wonder if he knows how many million miles he has flown since he started his training as a navy flyer.

In his senior year at Texas A&M College, he left school to do what he so long hoped to do — to become a flyer.

The army doctors rejected him because they thought his heart could not stand the strain, but they offered some hope when stating that he had spent too much study time; so he sought to build himself up by working as a roughneck in the oil fields, and after six months, he tried again. Then he got the message that he would never become a pilot.

However, with that determination which so often separates leaders from followers, George worked again to build himself up, and this time tried the navy. He was declared physically fit, and began his training, which led to his being commissioned ensign, in October 1941, and assigned to Squadron 8.

Shortly after that he was one of the eighty-odd pilots who formed sky cover and protection for the newly born ship *Hornet,* lying in the Atlantic near its birthplace, Norfolk Navy Yard.

Only an Appetizer

The author of this essay can offer this story as only an appetizer to those who want to know more about one of the most fascinating and heroic battle stories of all time, the battle of Midway — a battle over the possession and control of two little spots of sand, lying far out in the wastes of the Pacific Ocean.

After diligent research, and being rewarded by having the dramatic panorama spread out before me, I can only hope to stimulate enquiry on the part of men who honor men of valor, and know the price they pay for the protection of a nation and its people.

The fact that this surviving pilot is the son of my long-time friend, George H. Gay, Sr., and wife, makes me very anxious to draw a sketch which will revive a story that twenty-five years ago filled the front page of nearly every newspaper and magazine in America, and started the publication of many books that offer absorbing reading material. The generous loan of Mrs. Gay's collection of current papers, books and magazines, and her scrapbook, makes this effort possible.

Pilots on Carriers Are the Best in the World

Ernie Pyle tells of his feeling when he watched the pilots on the carrier. "The first time you see a plane land on a carrier, you almost die. At the end of my first day, my muscles were sore, just from being all tensed up, watching the planes come in. It is all so fast. Timing is so split second. Space is small. Somebody said that 'carrier pilots were the best in the world.' They must be, or there would not be any of them left alive."

Lt. Comdr. John Charles Waldron, leader of Squadron 8 aboard the carrier *Hornet,* was determined that the members of his crew would be just that, "The Best in the

World," if his training and driving force could make them that.

Before the finish of the shakedown cruise he had these young men flying in the morning, and flying in the afternoon, and doing skull work at night. He was a seasoned veteran, who knew that a man's life, and perhaps his ship's life, might depend upon a pilot's instant action, brought about from repeated exercise until it became automatic.

His crew was one of three on the *Hornet*, including fighters and bombers, just as the other two carriers were manned — the *Enterprise* with Torpedo 6, and companion groups, and the *Yorktown*, with its same complement of pilots, fighters and bombers.

The Turning Point in the War

In the fateful days of June 3, 4, 5, 6 and 7, 1942, the battle of Midway involved all three carriers, plus escort ships, and had the army and navy and marine forces on the tiny island, known as Midway.

And, before all that action was the planning by that gifted admiral, Chester Nimitz, and his cloistered code breaker, Comdr. Joseph Rochefort.

Only a book-length recital would begin to reveal the picture of this battle, how it was planned, how it was fought, and the fact that it reversed the course of history and marked the beginning of the end of Japan's rule of the Pacific waters.

Every phase of this historic event is an engrossing tale of heroic action — raw courage, blunders and luck, with a final answer, the turning point in the war, which had yet three years to run.

This story will chronicle the record of Torpedo 8, and the *Hornet*, but I hope someday to paint word pictures of the courage and fidelity of other actors in this drama.

The Japanese Dream

The war dream of Japan that resulted in the Pearl

Harbor blot on American arms did not originate overnight. More than sixty years ago, I heard the then navy hero, Lieutenant Hobson, tell us that someday Japan would certainly attack the United States. Their war lords were then planning for the accomplishment of that dream.

The Eagles Come Home to Roost

"On the day after Christmas, in the year 1941, just nineteen days after the horror of Pearl Harbor, the *Hornet* gathered her eighty-odd eagles underneath its eight hundred foot flight deck, to start on her shakedown cruise. . . ."

Capt. Andrew Mitscher, skipper of the *Hornet,* had under his command the newest war machine afloat, of studied excellence, and many of the men who were to man her had watched her during the gestation period; hence, they knew every bolt and beam from keel to bridge. But the crew to man her and the flyers who were to protect her and punish the enemy, were a mixed lot. Fifty percent of her pilots were trained veterans of the service, but many of them had never been in combat. The others were fresh out of Pensacola training. Many of the planes were obsolete.

A Happy Ship

The morale must have been high, for it was known, according to some writers, as "a happy ship," where relations between the command and the crew and the flyers were cordial and enthusiastic. All hands knew what a responsibility rested upon every fighting man, now that the cream of the navy lay in and near the waters of Pearl Harbor. The ships that were left had to overcome great odds against many seasoned Japanese forces, which had sunk two great British warships, and seemed to be roaming the ocean unchecked.

Army Planes Land on HORNET'S Deck

After a few weeks at sea, and undergoing constant

flight training by the pilots, and gunnery practice by the men who manned the ship's weapons, the *Hornet* came back to her birthplace, Norfolk, where the puzzled navy men saw two army flying ships dropped on her decks by big cranes. This caused much wonder and guesswork. The answer would come much later, when other land planes of the army were added to the group after the ship had gone through the Panama Canal and was based on the west coast.

Doolittle Comes Aboard

When at sea it was learned that the commander of this army group was Lt. Col. Jimmy Doolittle, and that he was Tokyo bound. Now came some ticklish timing. Doolittle had planned to leave the *Hornet* four hundred miles out of Tokyo, so as to put him over the city just at the right time for him to scoot across to a previously arranged landing place in China. But, when a warship of the Japs was sighted, the fear that Tokyo might be alerted caused a change of plans, even after our flyers had sunk the warship. Doolittle took off eight hundred miles out, which then caused the loss of men and planes which might have escaped had his original plans been carried out.

As soon as the Doolittle birds were gone, the *Hornet* started toward the Coral Sea, but too late to get engaged; so it was turned toward the fleet base. From there it was sent toward Midway.

The Battle of Brains

Now began the battle of brains. It was the responsibility of Admiral Nimitz to read the Japanese mind, and learn their battle plans. The Battle of the Coral Sea had left the *Yorktown* badly mauled. The Japanese were convinced that she had been sunk.

Deep in his code-breaking room, with double locked doors, Commander Rochefort ferreted out a word here and there from which he and his staff could estimate the enemy's move. With the aid of this occult gift of code breaking, the admiral was convinced that the enemy planned a double action. One, an attack on Dutch Harbor, in the Aleutians, and a three-pronged attack on Midway, these three groups being an attack group, a main force, and an occupation force coming from different directions. He estimated the time of the Japanese attack. At first, it was three days off, but was corrected to occur on June 3 and 4, 1942. Thus the forces on Midway could be ready to defend the island, and the fleet to attack.

YORKTOWN Restored

The *Yorktown* was so badly battered that the repair crew thought it would take weeks to restore her, but when the admiral said it must be ready in three days, the mechanics responded with the same patriotic loyalty as any man who wore the navy cloth; so the surprise package for the enemy admirals floated from the dry docks as the other ships steamed out of the harbor.

Search and Destroy

Now at last it became the duty of the U.S. Navy force to search and destroy, to concentrate on finding the enemy aircraft carriers, and sink or put them out of commission, leaving no ocean landing place for the enemy fighters to find resting place except in the bottom of the Pacific.

The brains at headquarters had worked out the timing of the Japanese forces accurately as to when they were expected to reach Midway, and Admirals Fletcher and Spruance had worked out plans to coordinate groups of flying squadrons to bring a mass action against the enemy. But, "The best-laid plans of mice and men ofttimes gang agley." The fifteen pilots of Torpedo 8 found themselves going alone.

According to the estimate of the time, distance, and speed of the Japanese forces, they would be in a certain distance and direction from Midway, and the plot plan was for our planes to drive for that projection point. After the enemy's planes spied the American forces, they headed in that direction instead of making another attack on the island. The forces of Midway had already put up a determined defense and had done much damage to the Japanese.

The battle plans of each opposing force was to surprise the other, and to concentrate on destroying the air carriers.

On the Wings of Destiny

While some of the forces of Torpedo 6 and part of the forces off the *Hornet* were driving toward the expected target area, Commander Waldron, anticipating the probable place and direction of the enemy, drove westerly, directing his men to hang on to his tail, and he would lead them right.

Some of the planes following the script, and with Commander Waldron smelling out the game, the plan of the coordinating attack did not materialize. The crew of Torpedo 8 did not know that they had air cover by Jim Gray, because Lieutenant Gray, piloting a fighter 6, thought he was covering a Torpedo 6, whose pilot had agreed to call, "Come on down, Jim," when needed. Jim Gray, twenty thousand feet among the clouds, did not know that the low-flying squadron 8 was in need of his help.

Skipper Waldron had been right. The great flotilla came into view. Ensign George Gay knew the hard decision his skipper had to make. Supporting planes were miles away. Waldron had to decide whether or not to make a suicidal attack along with his fifteen low-flying units. There were targets which they had been hunting: four of them. One, the *Soryu*, burning, and the big *Kaga* and *Akgi*, the last two, were believed by the Americans to be the carriers from which the Pearl Harbor attack was launched.

"Theirs Not to Reason Why — Theirs But to Do and Die"

Now had come the time to do what they knew had to be done, despite their slow planes, their inability to dodge the swarm of swift, skillfully manned Zeroes, despite the massed gunfire from the Japanese ships. A look into history reminds the reader of the charge of the Light Brigade. Many of the brigade rode back from the fiery furnace; only one of the fifteen pilots lived to tell the tale of this great sacrifice.

The only reporter of this scene was the wounded pilot, Ensign Gay. No T.V. machines, no flamboyant reporters, no Ernie Pyle to witness the last act except frightened Japanese who had other business on their schedules. The reams of accounts that filled the papers and magazines of that period, and even books written since then, can only repeat the story as remembered by the chief actor in this play. The detailed picture will not here be attempted, but the substance of the account will be given.

Pursuit Changed to Combat

All of a sudden, pursuit changed to combat, in which fifteen low-flying planes rushed toward the targets. Gay saw his skipper go down in a fiery drop of his plane. Then, in short order, one after another of his comrades disappeared. Then, his own plane fell after he had been shot in the left arm and in the leg. He had brushed the carrier *Kaga,* and swept across her bow. Now, despite his crippling wounds and the ship's disabled electrical system, he managed to discharge his torpedo, which he thought hit the target, as a great explosion followed the release of the pickle, as it was called. Ensign Gay heard his shipmate Huntington say, "I am hit," and Gay saw that he was dead. Huntington went down with the plane.

Gay went to work to save himself. As his plane sank, he pressed the slug out of his wounded arm, and bandaged his leg under water, after he found a floating cushion under which he hid to avoid being seen by enemy flyers who might strafe him.

All day long he had a hidden "fish eye" view of one of the most spectacular battles of the sea, when he was willing to watch the drama, as the American bombers now were giving the air carriers an awful pasting. They caught swarms of flyers refueling, and those in the air now had no place to land. The bombers were doing what the torpedoes, unprotected and alone, were unable to do. Gay saw the fleeing former masters of the sea, saw the flames and the smoke, and saw his comrades continue to blast the enemy. He saw many fall into the ocean.

A Night to Remember

With the coming of the night, he patched his rubber raft in order to find a place to rest. Not until late the next day, June 5, was he found and rescued, and taken to a hospital on Midway. Here his attending doctor asked him what treatment he had given his wounds. He said, "Soaked them in salt water for ten hours." Sixty planes had left the *Hornet* that morning of June 4, 1942. Twenty-four came back. Not one of the fifteen of Squadron 8. What became of pilot Gay, no one knew. Later, eleven more planes returned, adding to the twenty-four already reported. Yet, fifteen planes and fifteen pilots, and their fifteen tail gunners were not accounted for, until the report came of the rescue of Ensign Gay.

Except Huntington's name, the enlisted men's names are not given. The pilots' names are as follows: Lt. J. C. Owens, Jr.; Ensign E. L. Fail; Lt. Comdr. John C. Waldron; Lt. R. A. Moore; Ensign U. M. Moore; Ensign W. R. Evans III; Ensign G. W. Teats; Ensign H. J. Ellison; Lt. JG G. M. Campbell; Ensign W. W. Abercrombie; Ensign H. R. Kenyon, Jr.; Ensign George H. Gay; Lt. JG Jefferson Davis Woodwon; Ensign W. W. Cramer and Naval Air Pilot R. E. Miles.

No white crosses "row on row" mark their resting place, yet they should always find monument in the hearts of those who live in the land which they defended.

Back Home

Pic Magazine of November 10, 1942 carried a story by

Ensign Gay's father, George H. Gay, Sr., in which he related the exciting story of his first message from his son after the battle, and how he and his wife were pressed into going to the office of the local paper to receive the press reports as they came in. He told of the telephone calls with messages from everywhere inquiring about their son.

Captain Rickenbacker's Tribute

No other man in the world than Capt. Edward T. Rickenbacker is better qualified to know the meaning of the sacrifice made by the young men of the group called Torpedo 8. His tribute follows:

> To those boys should go the undying gratitude of every man, woman and child within the boundaries of the United States of America, for their daring and accomplishments, and loyalty to the cause that will go down in history as one of the outstanding epics of World War II. Few of us can visualize the strength of character and courage needed, and displayed by the members of Torpedo Squadron 8, in their willingness to help destroy a vicious enemy when death faced them.
>
> Let every American, man, woman and child, on the home front, try, in his humble way, to equal the efforts of these men, because none of us can ever hope to approximate their sacrifices.

One month after Ensign Gay was plucked from the sea, his parents had a visit from him. It is a moving story. Fortunately, he was able to return to duty, and in due season he became Lieutenant Commander Gay.

I did not know George Gay, Jr., but his father and I had long been friends. He was active in abstract work and in the oil business and farm mortgage work.

Pericles Oration on
Those Who Died in Battle

The following excerpt from the oration of Pericles, at the ceremony honoring those who died in battle, seems a fitting conclusion to this essay.

> They resigned to hope for their unknown chance of happiness. . . . But, in the face of death, they resolved to rely upon themselves alone, and when the moment came, they were reminded to resist and to suffer rather than to fly and save their lives. They ran away from the world of dishonor, and on the battlefield their feet stood fast. And, in an instant, at the height of their fortunes, they passed away from the scene; not of their fear, but of their glory.
>
> This empire has been acquired by men who do their duty, and had the courage to do it; who, in the hour of conflict, had the fear of dishonor always present with them. The whole earth is the sepulcher of famous men. Not only are they commemorated by columns and inscriptions . . . but engraven in the hearts of men.

In the Life of One Adult Person

What a yardstick is needed to measure the progress of air transportation during the adult life of one person is difficult to find. As one who has lived through that period, I am reminded that I was twenty-five years of age when the Wright Brothers made their maiden flight at Kittyhawk, North Carolina, in 1903. When our fellow townsman, Jerry Clark, landed his fighter plane in Captain McKinnon's cow pasture, in the edge of our home town, in 1917, I was then thirty-nine years old. And, now, on the twenty-first day of September, 1973, I read in our morning paper that the giant seven hundred and fifty passenger Concorde, a French-British make, rolled onto the runway of our greatest airfield in the world, between Dallas and Fort Worth. I had passed milepost 95.

References

I have searched through every book, magazine, manuscript and letter that I could obtain in order to tell this story. But, after absorbing all I could in thousands of pages, including contents of a giant scrapbook loaned me by Mrs. George Gay, widow of George Gay, Sr., the father of the central figure, Ensign George Gay, Jr., I can only list the various items consulted, yet not identify every source of quotes embraced in my recital.

A Ship to Remember, The Saga of the Hornet, Alex R. Griffin.
Incredible Victory, Walter Lord. Also other books.
The Navy Has Wings, Fletcher Pratt.
Men at War, Ernest Hemingway.
Free Men are Fight, Oliver Gramling.
The Story of America in Pictures, Allen G. Collins.
These Men Shall Never Die, Lowell Thomas.
American Navy in World War II, Gilbert Kant.
Victory Through Air Power, A. D. Versky.

The following items were returned to Mrs. George Gay, Sr. on April 22, 1968, after I had read them.

Main Scrapbook she had loaned me.
Oil Weekly, July 30, 1926, p. 99.
Framed picture of George Gay; letter, Admiral Nimitz, dated June 12, 1942.
Chicago Sunday Tribune, March 28, 1943.
Graphic, Chicago Tribune, June 25, 1949.
Argosy, p. 44, (date unknown).
Pic, November 10, 1942.
Graphic, June 20, 1948.
Graphic, June 27, 1948.
Graphic, June 19, 1949.

Graphic, July 18, 1948.
Graphic, July 4, 1948.
Graphic, July 23, 1948.
Graphic, p. 11, 1948, (month unknown).
Graphic, May 30, 1948.
Graphic, June 5, 1949.
Graphic, June 12, 1949.
Graphic, June 19, (year unknown).
Saturday Evening Post, March 26, 1949.
Saturday Evening Post, March 25, 1949 (?).
Kay Kaiser's Broadcast (Salute to son, Midway Island, July 1, 1942).
Life Magazine, April 30, 1942.
Life Magazine, February 12, 1946.

Copies of the picture loaned me by Mrs. George Gay, Sr. are included in this cover with the manuscript.

Small picture of the battle scene as interpreted by an artist, which was being hung in the city hall in Houston, with the Gay family looking on, and my good friend, W. A. Kirkland, who had been an officer in the Navy, in the Pacific.

Picture of George Gay, Sr., my friend and the father of Ensign Gay.

Picture of the pilots of Torpedo 8.

Picture of Mr. and Mrs. George Gay, Sr., and their hero son George and his sister.

I could not cite authorities for each statement which I may have borrowed, for after absorbing all the information I could through reading all these stories, I condensed the story as I remembered it.

Mrs. Gay approved the manuscript I wrote, so I believe I have avoided errors, even if the story does not meet the requirements.

Mr. Kirkland wrote me a letter of appreciation after I sent him a copy of the battle scene.